. . . airplanes, hallways, hotel kitchens. That was so much fun. Just to do it to see if you can get away with it. I'm always asked if we had sex in an elevator, as in the Aerosmith song. Sure, but on the other hand, I wouldn't be so bold as to think the song relates to me. I'm sure if he had sex with me in an elevator, he's probably done it with others, too. Sometimes I would listen to those songs and think, "Whoa! That's interesting! I wonder who that one is about . . ."

DREAM ON

Livin' on the Edge with Steven Tyler & AEROSMITH

CYRINDA FOXE-TYLER
and Danny Fields

BERKLEY BOULEVARD BOOKS, NEW YORK

DREAM ON: LIVIN' ON THE EDGE WITH
STEVEN TYLER & AEROSMITH

A Berkley Boulevard Book / published by arrangement with
the authors

PRINTING HISTORY
Dove Books edition / January 1997
Berkley Boulevard edition / September 2000

All rights reserved.
Copyright © 1997 by Dove Audio, Inc., and Cyrinda Foxe-Tyler.
Cover design by Pamela Jaber.
Cover photo by Larry Busacca/Retna Ltd.;
inset photo courtesy Cyrinda Foxe-Tyler.
This book may not be reproduced in whole or in part,
by mimeograph or any other means, without permission.
For information address: The Berkley Publishing Group,
a division of Penguin Putnam Inc.,
375 Hudson Street, New York, New York 10014.

The Penguin Putnam Inc. World Wide Web site address is
http://www.penguinputnam.com

ISBN: 0-425-17142-6

BERKLEY BOULEVARD
Berkley Boulevard Books are published by The Berkley Publishing Group,
a division of Penguin Putnam Inc.,
375 Hudson Street, New York, New York 10014.
BERKLEY BOULEVARD and its logo
are trademarks belonging to Penguin Putnam Inc.

PRINTED IN THE UNITED STATES OF AMERICA

10   9   8   7   6   5   4   3   2   1

CONTENTS

CONTENTS

DREAM
ON

PROLOGUE
Diving for Diamonds

I'll begin with the memory of a moment back in winter of 1979, when Steven Tyler and I were alone together on a Caribbean island. He was rich and famous, the lead singer of the awesomely successful American rock band Aerosmith, and I was his beautiful and pampered wife, partner, princess, master, and slave.

We had come to St. Martin on one of our periodic escapes from the grueling routine of being on the road. When a band is touring, you can only work so long before your body starts to give out. That year on the road, Aerosmith worked almost every single day—two or three days "on," then a travel day, then back to performing. Aerosmith worked harder than any band I've ever known in my life—three hundred and forty days of the year.

But now the band was in a time of crisis. Over the years drugs, drugs, and more drugs had sent the group into a scary decline. Just a few months earlier, lead guitarist Joe Perry, Steven's longtime partner, friend, and at times bitter enemy, had quit, followed by rhythm guitarist Brad Whitford. The album *Draw the Line* had been released in 1978, and though it reached number eleven on the *Billboard* charts, it was regarded as a disappointment both musically and commercially. There was still plenty of money, but the future did not look good. Steven and his managers, not a convivial crowd by that time, had to find replacements for Joe and Brad, and Steven was fried and badly in need of a vacation.

Our vacations were always on the islands, someplace hot where we could dig in the sand, parasail, scuba dive, snorkel, and lie in the sun. Steven was like a child at the beach. He loved it. These holidays were usually supposed to last only five days, but because it took that long just for Steven to unwind, I would fight to get ten days, and we'd end up able to spend about a week in the paradise of our choice. This time it was the French side of St. Martin. We flew first class and were driven by limousine to our very luxurious hotel, where we had the penthouse suite with balconies overlooking the sea and the gardens, linen draperies that billowed in the cool Caribbean breezes, and not one, but two sumptuous marble bathrooms.

Our baby, Mia, born just a year before, after we'd been married almost four months, was in New England, in the care of a local family.

Unlike when we were on tour, there were no bodyguards on vacations with us, because there were no fans on St. Martin. No teenagers could afford to be there. Of course, there was no one else from the

Aerosmith organization because the one purpose of taking the vacation was to get as far away from everyone else as possible. It was unheard of for any members of the band to spend holidays with one another, even in the best of times.

The night before, we'd had a horrible fight. Steven couldn't find his cocaine—it was stuffed in some shoe or pocket, he couldn't remember which—and he took it out on me. Everything, me included, was thrown around the hotel suite. I ended up cowering in a corner while he raged. He eventually found the blow, apologized, and promised me the next morning we would go shopping on the Dutch side of the island, where the stores were more exclusive.

The next morning our shopping excursion concentrated on skin care products, because our lily-white skin was about to be exposed to the rigors of the tropical sun, and we always overdid it. We bought nearly a thousand dollars' worth of oils and unguents, and it was all stashed in the trunk of our waiting limousine when we stopped to look in the window of a jewelry store. Prominently displayed was a gorgeous diamond and emerald bracelet. I gasped at the beauty of it and squeezed Steven's arm. He gave me a loving little smile and said, "Let's go. I need some sun."

We were in the sun for three hours, which turned out to be too long. At one point Steven went to get some food. We lunched and drank and even did drugs, ducking under beach towels for periodic snorts, sometimes coke, sometimes heroin. By late afternoon we looked and felt like two baked lobsters.

We went back to our room, and in separate bathrooms showered and smeared on a good proportion of the balms we'd purchased that morning. It would have been a great time for sex, but we were too burned to touch each other's ruby-red skin. There was an alternative to intercourse, however.

When I came out of my bathroom, Steven was lying on the bed with the sheet drawn up to his neck. "Kisses," he said.

That was our love code for a blowjob. It was my pleasure to give him pleasure, especially since *we'd* be avoiding the scorched parts of our bodies. I walked over to him and pulled the sheet down slowly. Circling his cock and balls was the bracelet from the store window, ninety-plus carats of crystalline fire.

"Dive for it," he said. "No hands."

I squealed a totally feminine and breathy little "Oooh!" and got down on my knees to retrieve the rocky treasure.

Steven loved getting—and giving—head. His cock was already hard when I unveiled it in all its gem-studded loveliness—seven inches long, circumcised, not too large a head, and small, smooth balls. A mouthful of hairy balls would have been a problem when you've got only your tongue, teeth, and lips with which to perform this delightful operation.

I started by ignoring the bracelet, opting instead for some tongue flicks, some suction, and some up-and-down lip action. Steven was a silent oral sex recipient—no "Suck that cock, baby!" or embarrassing moans and groans. But I knew he loved it; his whole body told me that.

The most exciting part was going to be me going for the bracelet, so I put that off until my love for Steven's penis had been properly demonstrated. Then, with my tongue, I began to poke around at the bracelet, mainly to see if the thing had been clasped shut (which would have presented some problems). Fortunately, only the tiny platinum safety chain was attached, so the bracelet was loose enough to slide off carefully, oh so carefully. I didn't want to scratch the swollen cock of America's foremost lead singer with anything so hard as a diamond.

Once the bracelet was removed and between my teeth, I placed it on the sheet between Steven's thighs, went back to his cock, and brought him off.

"I thought you'd like that," he said after he came. I didn't know if he meant the blowjob or the trinket, but I liked them both; I did indeed.

Within twenty-four hours of this love fest, I would be sporting a large pair of sunglasses and a white Hermès scarf to cover up two black eyes and the swelling elsewhere on my face. *Wow*, to be the number one woman of the number one man in American rock and roll: a man who was violent, cruel, and abusive one minute, generous, romantic, playful, and sentimental the next. So cruel that those closest to him couldn't believe it when he got lower than they thought possible; so romantic that he went way beyond any fantasy I'd ever had about the "guy of my dreams."

It was hard to believe I'd come this far. Nine years before that week in paradise, I'd thrown a cheap bag of clothing out of the second-story window of my stifling, horrible home in Oklahoma, and grabbed a ride to Austin with a couple of wild, out-of-town boys I hardly knew. My life as one of the 1970s' most glamorous and envied free spirits was about to begin.

ONE
Last Child

My real name is Kathleen Victoria, and I'm not going to give my last name because I want to leave my father out of this.

I was born in 1952 in Santa Monica, California. My mother was twenty-six when she had me, and I was her third and last child. She'd had her first, my brother, William Edward, when she was fifteen, and her second, my sister, Lynda, a year later. I was the child of my mother's second marriage. My parents divorced when I was two. I'd never seen very much of my father. When I was a teenager and the situation got too atrocious at home, I went to live with him and his wife, against my mother's wishes. My father is a real sleazebag. He'd been a sailor. All four of my mother's husbands had been in the service.

After my birth father, there was a third husband who came and went, and I remember next to nothing about him. I think he was a sailor, too, and he lasted two years. When I was six, Mom married for the fourth time, to a guy who was in the Air Force. This

man was a creep, and he was in my life until I left
home at seventeen.

Until husband number four entered the picture, the
man of the house was my brother, William Edward.
Twelve years older than me, with blond hair and blue
eyes, he was thin, beautiful, and very English-
looking, with gorgeous peach skin and heavenly
hands, and he was by far the most loving person in
my early life. William was good at wood-working,
and he made beautiful mahogany coffee tables with
rounded edges so I wouldn't hurt myself in case I
fell. He left home when I was in third grade and married his first girlfriend. He was only eighteen, and it
completely freaked my mother out. In the last thirty
years, I've seen him only a few times. He was always
so close to my mother; he never stood up to her.

My sister, Lynda, must have envied him getting out
of that hellhole, because she left right after that and
went to live with our biological grandmother, who
considered herself a genteel Southerner of ancient
lineage. She had long since disowned my mother because of her multiple marriages, and to her I didn't
even exist.

After my brother and sister left, I was devastated.
I had no friends to take their place, only my dog,
Ladybug. She smiled when she was happy—she really did—the only member of the household who
could or who had any reason to smile.

My mother was five foot nine and very attractive,
with blond hair and green eyes. She had been a model
once. She had really long legs, and I remember how

good she looked in the big skirts she always wore, especially the big orange one with poodles on it. A real fifties cliché, but one that I would learn to make use of later in the most trendy fashion circles in New York. But being trendy during those days was not foremost in my mind. I was much more concerned about the severe punishment that was ladled out by both my mother and stepfather. Of course corporal punishment was a much bigger part of parenting back then, but these two went overboard. So, of course, I got a bit rebellious and withdrawn.

My stepfather gave the word *pig* new meaning. He was short and stocky, with dark, curly hair. I think he was part American Indian. He was not emotional but very direct, and I always thought he hated me. In any case, he was always punishing me. How would it start? You name it. If I didn't walk at exactly the right pace and in just the right place, my mother would slap me really hard. If I spoke when I wasn't supposed to, I got smacked. Sometimes there didn't have to be any reason at all.

My stepfather got into it big time. He'd punish me if he didn't like the grades I was getting in school, or if I dropped a dish, because from the time I was ten, washing and drying all the dishes was my responsibility. I'd be in trouble if my teeth touched the fork while I was eating. This was my mother's idea of etiquette: Your lips take the food off the fork, not your teeth. I hated eating, but I did have perfect little manners.

I had been deathly afraid of my mother all of my

life. She was so strict, so proper, and so disturbed. It still scares me to think of those times. She'd just hit me on the street in front of all these strangers. *Wham!* Unbelievable! Imagine how embarrassing that is for a little girl.

In some ways I think he was beating me down to please my mother, but in other ways I think it made him feel powerful. Why do you want power over a child? I don't know, but it's a sick fucking thing. Maybe it took the place of affection in our home. I never saw my mother and her husband kiss or hold hands or show any tenderness toward each other.

I would learn about the sin of kissing from my mother; I suppose she wanted to nip that activity in the bud before I got into playing Post Office or Spin the Bottle. But it's not like she said, "Sweetie, do be careful of those nasty kissing games." What she did say was, "If I ever find out you've done anything like that, I will *kill* you." *Kill*, that's the word she used, and I believed her. Kissing was the filthiest thing a person could do, and in my house it would earn me the death penalty.

My mother had practically no friends, and no one in her family spoke to her. Her main activity was cooking meals every day, and her life revolved around church. I don't know what she got out of it. She had left the Catholic church, which I'd been born into, and tried Lutheran and Southern Baptist and a bunch of others, as if she were looking for something. Now she's a born-again Christian. She really believes

Jesus is going to come back and get us for being bad. I have news for you, Mom: *Jesus is dead, he's not going to come back and get anybody*.

Whatever she's looking for, I know she still hasn't found it. These days we talk every now and then, and she still seems to be searching. She's long since left my stepfather. Thankfully, she got rid of that fucker a few years ago. I have never met a more despicable creature. Because he was in the Air Force, we moved around a lot from the time that my mother married him, when I was six, to when I finally escaped at seventeen. During the years with him, we lived in Spokane, Washington, Klamath Falls, Oregon, and then the Philippines. I was always leaving what few friends I had made, and worse than that, my mother made me leave my pets behind. I had to leave them on the doorstep. It was horrible driving away and leaving these little creatures. I was very into animals. You can look into the eyes of a dog or a cat, and it looks back at you with so much soul. I had one dog that used to run with me through the woods in Washington State. I would pretend I was Sheena, Queen of the Jungle.

My stepfather, U.S. Military Hero that he was, wore a uniform most of the time, and whenever he had it on, he walked like a goddamn rooster. He acted like it added something to his aura. To me he looked like an asshole in and out of the uniform.

I have to be fair to my mother. There are some good things about her. For one thing, even though she was a military wife, and could trace her family back before the Revolution, there wasn't a hint of snobbery about her. To this day, she is one of the most democratic people I've ever known. I've never known her to judge people by their race or social status. I've got to give her credit for that. I don't know where it came from. Considering what a horror she is on every other level, it's almost an accident that she is so without prejudice.

And there are things I admired. For instance, she loved music and clothes, and those were the two things that saved my life—made my life, really. My mother loved Chuck Berry. "Roll Over Beethoven" was her favorite record of all time. She had worn out a couple of dozen 45's of "Roll Over Beethoven" by the time I was a teenager. She also loved Frankie Laine, which is pretty cool, considering it could have been Perry Como, Julius LaRosa, Frank Sinatra, or Eddie Fisher.

My brother also loved music. He had the most amazing record collection, which he left behind when he eloped. When he was still at home he played this music all the time with no complaints from the grown-ups. Am I describing the House of Contradictions here? Kid beaters, music lovers—that's the way it was.

The Coasters, the Platters, Fats Domino (whom I thought was the most beautiful man who ever lived), and the covers of all those records! The black girls were always so pretty, and they had such beautiful hairdos and clothes, especially the girl vocalist in the Platters. I think that's when I started becoming obsessed with clothes. I often think about how naive I was about racism. First of all, I never saw any real black people in all the places we lived. They were just these beautiful creatures with beautiful clothes who sang beautiful music and got their pictures on record covers. I'm not saying I wanted to be black, I never would have thought of that, but I certainly did think these people were from heaven and had wonderful lives, far more wonderful than mine.

And then came Elvis. In 1957 we were still living in Santa Monica. My sister, Lynda, took me shopping and bought me these little pedal pushers that had record discs on them. And my first 45 that I picked out myself was "Teddy Bear." To this day I think there's something contagious about the hysteria that fans have for their idols, and like my sister, I caught Elvis-hysteria. She was crazy for him. I think she went as far as having fainting spells. In turn, my brother would make fun of Lynda's hysteria, and because I worshiped him, I joined in picking on her. Still, I caught it. By the time I was five, I could do a pretty good Elvis impersonation.

The songs I listened to meant more to me than anything I ever saw on television or read in books. They were all about relationships, heartaches, and happiness, things I could relate to or wanted to relate to. Because my brother and sister had had this fabulous collection, when they fled the persecution of our house, all their records became mine.

My first real teen idol besides Elvis was Luke Halpin from *Flipper*. I was as temperamental, sensitive, and emotional as any pubette could be, but Luke Halpin was my guy. He was tan and adorable, and he wore little surfer shorts and was so cute. And he wasn't much older than me, so I thought he was perfect. My fantasy with Luke—I guess it's every young girl's presexual fantasy—was just to be in the same room with him. You know, dancing, going to a party, your dream date with Luke Halpin.

When I was twelve, my mother, her fourth husband, and I moved to the Philippines. I had to leave school, friends, and pets behind, and move ten thousand miles to a strange country. It sounds like it might have been an exotic experience, but it really wasn't. We were in a compound with only Americans— American military personnel and their American kids.

I was at the age where boys were becoming interesting, but I was still afraid of them. I didn't look at them sexually. They were like big brothers, kind of like my own darling big brother, whom I still adored and missed so much. And most of what I knew about guys, or thought I knew, came from music. These guys who wrote and sang the songs were giving me information along with the music. They were falling in love, breaking up, and falling in love again, and I was learning what everything meant by listening to their songs.

No one at home told me anything. I couldn't talk to my mother, that's for sure. She was pulling this health number back then, where she seemed to be suddenly stricken with a series of mysterious diseases. She was always at the doctor's office, and around the house there was a gigantic array of pills and medications. I could be really sick and wouldn't be allowed to go to the doctor, but she always seemed to be at the doctor's office whenever she wasn't doing something churchy. Besides being sick and religious, she was really moody. Oregon, California, the Philippines—it could have been the damn moon, but it was still like a portable Nazi youth camp wherever I was with my mother and her loathsome husband.

Then, all of a sudden, the Beatles came out, and the world changed completely. Other girls went nuts over the Beatles, and I sort of went along. I always thought they were goofy-looking, like cartoon characters, and their music was like cartoon music. It had no depth. But the girls were going mad, and everyone bought their first album, and I wanted it because everyone else had it. I had to make myself this way because this was the way the rest of the pack was going, but I really didn't like it. I didn't understand it. The music was nothing like I knew, but I just wanted to be a part of the crowd. The Beatles bonded us. All the girls were buying Beatles bubble gum cards, and I did, too, because it gave me the chance to get out of my sick house.

So I was into the Beatles "thing," but I've got to tell you that I was never impressed with them musically. I was a little rocker, and they were just too white-bread for me. I'd been brought up listening to all this fifties stuff, and to me the Beatles' songs and attitude were kind of wimpy. But still, if you were a kid in 1964, you were swept away by the whole British Invasion thing, and there was no doubt that it was led by the Beatles. But shortly after that the Rolling Stones came out, and I completely fell in love with them. They were like the coolest guys in the whole wide world. I thought Mick was really cute. "Satisfaction," 1965. It was mad. These were the guys. They sounded like the old music. The sound was there, the beat was there, and they did it great. The Beatles didn't do anything great, except *be* the Beatles. They just jumped and shouted and wore little cartoon clothes. But the Rolling Stones were making music I could relate to. It recalled the Chuck Berry stuff I'd loved and all the black music I'd grown up with. I knew where they were coming from.

Back then, anything English was new and great. Herman's Hermits, the Dave Clark Five, the Kinks—oh God, the Kinks, I loved them. The Kinks and the Rolling Stones were *it*. The Kinks were so cool, and Ray's eyes are still kooky. I'll always love them. Many years later, I found that rock-and-roll musicians, I mean the hard, loud, and fast ones, the kind I always hung around, were themselves attracted to girls who in the sixties preferred the Stones over the Beatles. In fact, I can say the Beatles girls went nowhere, while the Stones girls moved right into the big time.

For my mother the Beatles were harmless, although she hated all of the hysteria. But the Stones sent her over the edge. "Those Rolling Stones are from hell!" she'd scream. "They're from hell, and if you listen to them, that's where you'll end up!" I think she really believed that (there are people just as nutty in the world today bringing up teenage children, so I've heard), but her hatred of it only made me listen to the Stones even more closely, because I was paying a price for it. She'd beat me if she found me listening to a Stones song; she could spot that sound from hell in a few seconds.

Keith Richards was the Rolling Stone I loved. I was obsessed with a boy in my school who I thought looked like Keith Richards. He became my "boyfriend." I don't remember his name. I was in the fifth grade and he was in the seventh, and he was trying to look mod. He was trying so hard to look like Keith. Everything was Mick, Mick, Mick, but for me Keith was the cool one.

Oh, the boys back then. They were either mod or preppy. The preppy ones had madras shorts and Bass Weejun loafers. There was a teen club, and we could dance there. We twisted. That's when I first started making out. I loved making out, because I knew my mother would hate it if she knew I was doing it, but let's be real; it felt great. Finally I had something physically, emotionally, and sexually interesting in my life. The guys were shy, and you just sort of kissed in the schoolyard. It was far from heavy stuff, and I just loved it. If my mother had ever found out, she would have killed me. I can see it as clear as day. She would have grabbed me by the hair, humiliated me, and dragged me into the house to beat me.

Even then I was cultivating a sense of humor to get me through all the bullshit. That's what gets peo-

ple out of bad situations. You go either one way or
the other. I'm really glad I've been able to see the
humor and irony in everything that's happened to me.
No life is easy, but if you're born with a little bit of
ham and a little bit of creativity, it sure helps.

Speaking of humor, one thing we did that was kind
of sexy in my early teenage years was called "grind-
ing." You'd stand there kissing and grind your pelvises together. There was no arm or hand touching,
just lips and pelvises. It was a whole sensation of
actually coming in contact with another human body
that was far removed from playing ball or tag or
something. It was really enlightening, feeling another
person's energy.

Some of the girls would go further. They would get
fingered. I thought that was the scariest thing in the
world. These were the girls who wore eye makeup,
too, and tight pants. They had big hair. I wouldn't
call them sluts, but they were just short of being sluts.
I was a real prude about it, and the girls who did it
made a point of talking about it in front of me just to
torture me, because I'd get so flustered. I think there
must have been a few who went even further, but no
one talked about that. They did talk about getting fingered—that was a mark of pride and maturity. You'd
be in the bathroom putting on lipstick (which I had
to wipe off before I went home), and there were these
girls talking about getting fingered.

I didn't know what it meant. I had to be told.
They'd laugh and giggle about whether it was one
finger or two fingers. Two fingers was big time. No

one ever talked about giving head. I don't know if anyone even knew what a blowjob was. And then I'd hear the boys say something like "She was so wet," and I had no idea what that meant, so I had to go back to the girls and ask them.

The boys talked about masturbating all the time. The girls would listen, and their eyes would bug out. Boys were starting to play with themselves a lot at that age, and so the word *masturbate* was a big word that would scare girls. I couldn't visualize it at all. I didn't even know what a penis looked like. Even my pet dogs had all been females.

The closest I ever got to a cock was when I sort of touched one. This was a couple of years later, when I was fifteen. The guy was seventeen and looked a little like Keanu Reeves, only with more fair coloring. He was tall with beautiful brown-golden hair, and he was in a band. He was a close friend of my girl-friend's brother, and she and I sneaked out one night and went down to where this band was playing in their button-down Brooks Brothers shirts and chinos. We had on little lamé T-shirt dresses and flowers painted on our legs, eye makeup, and ironed hair. After the show, I was making out with this guy behind a shed, and he took my hand and put it down his pants, and oh God, I just freaked out.

I remember exactly how it felt. First of all, it was a long cock, because my fingers touched it before they hit any pubic hair. It was hard, but not hard like wood, more like a warm cucumber. Smooth and dry except for one wet sticky spot. I didn't know what to do. I just froze and freaked. I yanked my hand out and ran away, and I practically ran right into a police car that had been cruising around. The cops saw these under-age kids at two in the morning. My girlfriend and I were taken down to the police station and we had to call our parents. I was beaten and grounded for life. The police said, "Oh, we won't tell your parents what you were doing just before we found you." I think they'd seen the hand in the pants and figured I'd been giving him an energetic whack, but it wasn't a hand job. In fact, it wasn't even a pinky job.

I scrubbed my hand for hours. I was wild with anxiety. I used Comet and really hot water, and got dish-pan hands. My earliest attempt at birth control. What's more, I could never talk about that with the other girls. I probably told my cat or my dog, and I probably told God. "I'm so sorry, God." I was one of those. The guy with the penis wasn't a boy, he was a pre-man, and I was much too innocent. Actually, he'd been very nice about it, very gentlemanly. He just gently took my hand and put it down his pants, and my hand came out carrying a peculiar new substance.

Eeeww!! I think he knew I wasn't going to be much fun, even though he was trying to get some real action. And then he turned out not to be such a gentleman after all; he told my girlfriend's brother that I'd given him a hand job, and I never heard the end of it. "You're so stupid!" he had said. I never knew what he meant by that. Because I did it? Because I didn't do more? Because I didn't do it very well? Probably all of the above.

Boy, what goes around really does come around. When my daughter, Mia, became sexually active, she just did what she wanted to do when she wanted to do it. It was difficult for me to cope with that. I had to be a mom and scream, "You're too young!" and then I'd get angry and say, "Now, let's not get angry about this." Naturally, I was trying to be the opposite of how my own mother would have been, yet still provide "guidance" and "wisdom." As if.

It was a nightmare, all totally new for me, sitting down like the big boss with my teenage daughter. And she's going, "Well, this is not really cool, us talking about this." And I said, "But I thought I taught you better than that." Where and when I would have taught her this Better Behavior I really don't know, but you like to think your great sensibilities have been transmitted somehow. Even though you know you're not exactly a superb role model, you think you're a terrific transmitter of wisdom. Guess again. On the other hand, I have to add that I'm proud of her, and she's a fine, loving person, and I guess it didn't kill her that she started having sex. It killed *me* that she did, but not her.

I wanted to take Mia to the Whitney Museum for this retrospective of Warhol movies directed by Paul Morrissey, and my girlfriends, now the stars of some of these extremely sexually oriented pictures such as *Heat* and *Flesh*, would yell, "You can't take your child to see me tying a ribbon around Joe D'Alessandro's cock!" I would say, "Oh please, get over it. This is a hip kid. She knows what goes on."

Here were these goddesses of the 1960s women's sexual liberation, warning me about exposing my daughter to ribbons around a cock. These were girls who gave blowjobs on the sofa at Andy Warhol's Factory during business hours, with people watching and cheering them on like the champions they were.

TWO
War Days

It was so goddamn hot in the Philippines, except for the monsoon, when there would be nine days of nothing but rain. There were lizards running around the house all the time, and sometimes the really big ones would chase you. And there were always people looking in through the windows. I guess they were Filipino spies or something. But all I did was hang out, go to school, and go swimming. My friends were army kids who'd be there two years maximum. Then they'd be gone, out of my life—just like that.

I hated the whole military thing. I had to make my bed in a military way or get beaten. Not surprisingly, I was hating my parents more and more. They were so unenlightened. When Vietnam and the antiwar movement were escalating, they were real "love it or leave it" about America. My mother was out of her mind, extremely right wing and ultraconservative. All my parents could see on the horizon was drugs and long hair, and for them it was the doom scenario. Forget about noticing anything of artistic value in

what was happening in the sixties. For the first time
in history, my peers and I were getting the message
that there were possibilities for change. Meanwhile
my parents thought the world was coming to an end.

The compound we lived in was a waystation during
the war in the Philippines. I was thirteen or fourteen
at the time. I'd see the blue bus with the red cross on
it and young boys with bloody casts on their arms
and legs passing through. The ones who were
wounded too seriously to be treated in Vietnam were
flown to the hospital at Clarke Air Force Base near
us. They were really a mess. It was an awesome revelation for me. These boys, coming back in pieces,
not old enough to drink, vote, or have long hair, but
old enough to get their heads blown off. I started to
think of America as a giant death factory. I actually
remember being in the kitchen at a girlfriend's house,
and her parents were entertaining General Westmoreland! The Monkees were on the TV, and General
Westmoreland was there with all these colonels and
they were all complaining that they could have ended
the war really easily, if only the goddamn politicians
would have let them be the total soldiers they really
were cut out to be.

So everything I knew about grown-ups seemed
wrong and ugly and awful and everything I knew
about kids seemed innocent and beautiful. Boys not
in the service had long hair and played guitars. Boys
in the service had those godawful military haircuts
and were missing parts of their bodies.

About this time I became obsessed with the girls

in the music fan magazines. Not like Annette Funicello, but the fabulous English girls, the "birds" of London, who were going with the English rock stars, like Anita Pallenberg and Patti Boyd. These girls were so divine and wore the hippest clothes. Every one of them had *the* look. And they were with those cool guys who made great music. I found these girls absolutely superior. I never questioned anything about them or thought that they might have any problems. I truly believed they were happy all the time and never cried, just wore beautiful clothes, listened to records, and went shopping on Carnaby Street. This was La-La Land in my mind. If you had told me then that I would one day be one of those rock-star girlfriends I'd have fainted, at the very least.

I guess this was the time I started getting "serious" with boys, which meant making out, holding hands, and even going steady—all unbeknownst to my parents, of course. Mike Stanton was my first love. He was the most beautiful boy in the whole world. His father was a major in the Air Force, and he was the most divine creature that ever lived. I still remember him as being the best boyfriend I ever had in my life. He was five feet eleven inches, with brown hair, blue eyes, and the most perfect skin. When we met, I was in the eighth grade and he was in the tenth.

I wasn't allowed to date and definitely not allowed to get into a car with anyone, but my mother made an exception for him because he was so well-groomed and well-mannered, to the point of being almost chivalrous. Also, since we were both on the swimming team at school, I was allowed to drive to practice with him in his car. If it were just any male, I would have been completely forbidden from getting into a car with him, but since he was taking me to practice and was so polite, it was okay. Once we were going to a swim meet on the bus and my skirt split up the back. He was so sweet. He walked right behind me so no one could see my panties. He did it in a very protective way, no giggles, no leering. He just adored me, and I loved him. Even today I'm still in love with him.

He'd take out his retainer, and we'd lie down and French kiss. He'd put his hand between my legs and then go, "Uh oh, I can't do that yet. I'll wait for you to be old enough." Whatever he said was God's word. I wanted more. I wanted him to finger me. I wanted all of him. Mike Stanton was just purity personified. I know he had gone all the way with other girls, but he treated me like someone he would never defile. He did give me my very first hickey. My mother was not happy about it. When she found his bracelet after digging around my bedroom for telltale evidence, she wanted me to give it back to him, but I said no way.

He was so beautiful and smart, well bred, kind, and genteel. He was not judgmental of anyone, never said a dirty or an unkind word, and had a baby-blue Volkswagen bug that was shipped over from America. I think he had slept with a girl I knew, because she kept threatening to beat me up. She was older than me, and I was afraid of her. But Mike took care of it. He never let anything get in the way of our love.

I don't know what he said to her, but she apologized to me and was always nice to me after that.

We went out for less than a year until he had to go back to the States. I remember how it ended. It was the most painful parting in my life. He sent me a letter while I was still living in the Philippines, and he said that he was joining the Army to put in two years. We'd always been so antiwar, so anti the whole military thing, and I couldn't believe he would do that. My girlfriends and I were sitting there reading this letter, and I was crying my heart out, "How can he do this?" I was so afraid he would get killed.

I wrote him back a terribly cruel letter saying I hated him, that I never wanted to speak to him again. I never heard from him again. But gosh, he was gorgeous, and the best kisser in the whole world. I've never loved anyone the way I loved him.

So I was in the Philippines, wildly in love with Mike Stanton, and at the same time I was having all these fantasies about being a nun. That's right. Being a nun was my childhood dream, from day one, the earliest ambition of Miss Sex&Drugs&Rock&Roll. I had been born Catholic, and before my mother did one of her many church switcheroos, I had been to some Catholic schools. I was going to be a nun, a member of the Poor Clare's order (Claire is my Christian name), and I thought they were wildly appealing because they had no clocks, just bells that tell the time, and they grow their own food, rely on handouts, do charity work. The purity of it was spiritual to me, to be so simple and minimalist; I think I might find that same simplicity and benevolence in Zen Buddhism, if I ever get into the practice of it.

Anyhow, you're probably all snickering by now: "Yeah, she begins her life story with a memory of a blowjob, but in her heart of hearts she's a saintly nun." Well, I happen to be a deeply spiritual person, not bogus religious like all that "Christian" hate-filled bullshit, but really spiritual. Back then in the Philippines, though, I had to pursue my Catholicism on my own. In a country that's primarily Roman Catholic, it was not difficult to find catechism classes. The other thing I pursued was etiquette. Wherever there are military schools, there are "deportment" classes, and I ate that stuff up. This was way beyond what my mother had taught me, this was the real thing, like how to eat a meal with three separate-sized forks. I loved it. I still set a fabulous table. And if you did well in those classes, you were invited to have dinner with visiting politicians and dignitaries. It was my first taste of the VIP treatment I'd get later, when I was on the rock-and-roll A-list.

I don't like to think that I was a social-climbing teenager; it's just that the kids I was closest to just happened to be the kids of the highest-ranking officers. (You'll always find me in the best circles, and it's not like I try.) These officers' kids lived in formal homes unlike anything I'd ever seen. Their mothers changed outfits about four or five times a day, and so did the servants—from pink outfits in the morning to black in the evening! Our maid wore the same muu-

muu all day long, so you could tell we weren't in the higher echelon.

There was a very rigid class consciousness that applied especially to the soldiers. I mean, never mind the natives, they were invisible nonhumans, but the soldiers, being American and English-speaking and young (and occasionally adorable!), were completely off limits. We weren't allowed to talk to them. I had a girlfriend who got pregnant by one, and she vanished off the face of the earth. They weren't allowed to talk to us, either, and it was very sad. From my backyard you could see the injured boys being brought in, and all you're supposed to do is wave at them and be really cute and American. Waving to them was your patriotic duty, but talking to them, forget it. Talking to soldiers was like rolling in shit. I mean, that's what you were taught. The war is good and the soldiers are doing a good thing, but don't mix with them, even though they're doing this wonderful thing to protect us. I wasn't stupid enough to buy into that crap, though, because if you're seeing death all the time, you have to ask yourself, "How wonderful is war?"

All the caskets! We lived near a warehouse, and we could see thousands of aluminum caskets, all stacked and empty. I had to ask my parents what they were. The caskets were being shipped to Vietnam, or else used for the wounded boys who came to the Philippines and didn't survive. It was really scary for all of us, but especially for the boys I knew who were the sons of the officers and ambassadors. They'd see these kids their own age, wounded or headed for the casket supply, and they'd think, *This could be me*.

We didn't talk about it much, but we hated this war. The kids whose fathers were high-ranking officers had to be really careful not to say anything against the war, because the parents were responsible if the kids did anything "unpatriotic." From what I saw of the antiwar movement back in America in the seventies, the antiwar sentiment was just as powerful back then in the sixties among the children of the men who were literally calling the shots in the Land of Death. Only it was unspoken, because you would be bringing disgrace down on your whole family if you said what you really thought about the whole disgusting mess.

We were in the Philippines for about three years and returned to the States in 1967. When I got back I decided I wanted to live with my biological father in Orange County. My mother hated him, but she couldn't stop me from visiting him.

My biological father, his new wife, and their two daughters lived in a nice house that was very California-looking. His wife was a pretty Italian woman, petite, dark hair, very Gina Lollobrigida, in black toreador pants decorated with rhinestones that sparkled when she moved. Right after I moved in with them, they moved out of the nice house into an apartment complex in Santa Ana. This was no longer cool. I had to sleep on a tiny fold-out bed with the two girls. I guess my father had lost all his money, but besides that, the vibes were unpleasant on every level.

My stepmother did not need a sexually blossoming teenager around her own daughters, who were seven and ten.

This was about the time I felt the New York bug coming. I started to feel that everything was happening in New York. *Eye* magazine, long since defunct, had made a big impression. I knew the clothes were hipper on the East Coast, and that was always very important. People looked hipper. New York had that edge, at least from what I could tell of it from afar. I loved the way it looked in pictures, especially all those little skyscrapers.

I still didn't have breasts at fifteen. Some girls did. The girls with the biggest boobs were the coolest girls, but it was the time of Twiggy, so skinny girls with little boyish haircuts were okay. Still, I wanted boobs. Let's face it, you know that guys want girls with boobs, no matter what's trendy. Not that I was hanging out with that many guys, but I was sneaking into rock-and-roll shows, and that's when I discovered the beauty of speed.

Speed was the basic household drug at the time, because everyone's parents were taking huge amounts of it as part of their "weight control" efforts. If you were an overweight adult in the 1960s, doctors prescribed amphetamines, and children would snitch them and go to school buzzing. Consequently I had a friend with a steady supply of biphetamine sulfate, "black beauties." My father and stepmother knew I was on something and didn't want their young children around this buzzing whacko (I was only moderately whacko, but when you're fifteen, it shows up all over the place). You're a kid, you don't think, and you don't realize you're high and acting it. My stepmother was getting very uptight, and she was very strict. I don't remember any laughter in that house. My father was hardly ever home but kept getting phone calls from other women. And they both knew I was getting high on speed, so before I even turned sixteen I got sent back to my mother in Oklahoma. Altus Air Force Base was to be my new home. It's the home I ran away from, and though I would come back for a little while, it was to be my last home with any parent of either sex, ever.

THREE

Deep in the Heart of Texas

By the time I rejoined my mother and stepfather, I no longer wanted to become a nun. Rock-and-roll culture had taken firm root in my imagination, and my major role model became Jane Asher, Paul McCartney's girlfriend. She took the place of Marianne Faithfull, Patti Boyd, and Anita Pallenberg. Jane was gorgeous, but when I discovered peroxide, I went for the Patti Boyd look. Marianne Faithfull was a double idol because she sang in addition to going out with the guys.

Girl singers weren't wild until Janis Joplin came along. Meanwhile, the boy singers were wild, and the girls were like fabulous still photographs. Janis Joplin changed my idea of what a woman in rock and roll could be. I was crazy about her. I thought she was pretty, and she had the best laugh. How could you not love her? She was the cutest thing in the world; so hip, with this amazing voice. You may not believe this, but as fascinated as I was by the rock-and-roll world, I never wanted to sing rock. I wanted to be an opera star. I couldn't wait for my mother to leave the house so I could sing opera. I just sort of trilled and screeched. I always thought it had something to do with that stash of Mediterranean blood in me making itself known, because I've never gotten over it.

But back then, I was stuck in Altus, Oklahoma, as far from fabulousness as possible. Still, I was determined to make the best of it. I decided to get in with the cool kids in the town. Now, kids those days didn't usually make friends with the kids on the Air Force base, because they're not going to be around too long. Somehow, though, I got myself a passable Oklahoma accent, the right hairdo (a good, short hairdo was incredibly crucial to your social success in Altus), joined the Girls' Club, and went out with the cutest boys.

The elite girls were from the oil and banking families. They had better clothes, cars, and hair, and the best-looking boys in tow. I think the hair was more important than the oil and the boys. If you didn't have frosted hair, you just didn't have hair. It didn't matter what color your hair was, those were the sixties, and you had to have frosted hair. Professionally frosted—girlfriends weren't doing it for you then. All the boys had Pontiac GTOs, and a hot night out was hamburgers at Clyde's, though at the time I was dating a guy who was driving his father's Lincoln, which was embarrassing.

Friends called me Skip, because I looked like Barbie's little sister Skipper. Oklahoma was very flat and windy and got very cold. And while the landscape and life made me feel like this all-American girl on the outside, my perky exterior was covering a deep, painful, and longing soul. I was reading the Koran and lots of poetry, and I could feel the rocks crying. How's that for adolescent enlightenment?

But where was I? I was in Prairie Land, so far away from everything, with my mother, hating school, and it all sucked, with an exception or two.

I think I lost my virginity in Oklahoma. I'm not sure exactly what happened, but it hurt, so I mark that moment as the loss of my maidenhood. The boy's name was Wesley. He was gorgeous. If I say Ethan Hawke, will you get the picture? He was cool. His sister got pregnant and had to go away to one of "those" places, and it was very hard for him, and he got into fistfights over it all the time. He had a really good attitude and was really caring, with blue eyes and light brownish red hair, not big.

We were making out at his house. He was homesick that day so I went to visit him, because I liked him and had to know what was wrong. We started to do IT, and it hurt, so we stopped, but I knew he got it in there a little. I was dressed while this happened, and I don't think I even took my panties down. I couldn't have handled that. I guess they got moved aside a little. There's no way your clothes come off at that age. I was in my twenties before I could be naked with a guy.

Well, according to what my religion taught me, I'd been ruined, but I really didn't care. I never worried about not being able to "give" myself to a husband some day. That stuff sounded like bullshit to me from day one. I was worried that it hurt, because I liked it and I wanted to do it, and I didn't know why it was hurting, I didn't like this problem, so it was probably six months before I ever did it again. I couldn't talk about the first time with anyone, because it's the kind of thing that changes you, and I wasn't tough enough to get in the game with the tough girls who have sex and talk about it. I always thought they would have made fun of me. And besides, I was starting to get the feeling that it was time to go. It was 1969 and I was just seventeen, but I wanted out of the life I was living. It was God's will.

I didn't care how it was going to be done, but I do remember a critical moment. My stepfather hit me and started ranting about my mother making the biggest mistake of her life by having me. This, by the way, was not a spontaneous revelation on his part but had been learned from my mother herself: "You were a mistake!" was one of her constant picker-uppers.

Anyhow, that evening I'd been secretly planning to hang out with these two guys. It was neither a sex thing nor a social thing. They weren't part of my crowd. I'd only known them for a few months. They were Easy Rider kind of guys, a little older than me. But instead of just walking out the front door and meeting them on the street in front of my house, I went up to my room, put on my new shoes, stuffed $25 into my purse, packed a little bag, signaled to the two guys standing below in the yard, and threw the bag out the window. Then I walked out, mumbling something to my parents about a Girls' Club meeting. I told the guys I was running away, and they said, "Cool. Let's hitchhike to Texas." And I was outta' there.

There were a lot of lucky things at work for me at that moment. For one, the two guys never even tried to touch me, so there was no problem there. I mean, I would have let them, probably, if it meant the difference between getting away or not. And two, even though I lost my wallet in Texas and the police found it and notified my parents of my likely whereabouts, my mother made no effort to get me back. She was as happy to see me gone as I was happy to have left home.

It's easy for me to say now that I would have responded if either of those guys had come on to me sexually. These guys were like my delivering angels. And before long I did learn that every now and then getting fucked was the price you paid for freedom, if you were a teenage girl living off the kindness of strangers.

When you're a new girl on the street, everybody wants a piece of you. You want to hang out with other kids, but they're all in the same position. The ideal situation was to make friends with kids who lived at home and stay with them for a while. You know, your friend tells her parents, "Oh, she goes to school with me, she's coming over to spend the night," or "She's going to spend a few days here while her parents are out of town." Kids lie—we were good at it then, and they're good at it now.

After a while it became clear to me that I was expected to put out if I wanted a place to stay. I mean, that's what I did in those days. I needed a place to stay, and the host was a little horny, so I did it. It was never my number one choice, but I did it. If I couldn't stay at a friend's house or afford a hotel, I paid for my room with the nice, warm, slippery holes that God gave me. To say the least, innocent as it seemed, I'm not thrilled with the memories of those times.

It always began with a friend saying, "Oh, you can stay at this guy's house, he's really nice. Don't worry about it, it'll be all right." And I stayed there, and the guy gave me some food or got me stoned or something, and then he started the party. Maybe I didn't want to party. After all, I was just looking for a place to sleep, but what choice did I have?

To me these situations always smacked of rape, not horrible rape where you're grabbed off the street by a predator who might kill you, but rape just the same. There are different degrees, of course, and obviously some are more scary and heinous than others. But the indoor predator variety is a rapist, too, because he was someone you were supposed to trust. Each time it was different, and yet it was always the same, because it was uninvited. Someone was on top of me, and I couldn't get him off. I couldn't get away, and I didn't cry; it's like being beaten as a child. With guys like these it's always the power trip. And then they have the balls to say how great I was. Thanks! Obviously it's not cool to put myself in that position, but when I was seventeen, I had a lot to learn.

So my guardian angels and I made our first stop in Lubbock, Texas, where I met other kids who were also on their own. I stayed at different people's houses. After a few months I went to Austin, and that was rough, because there was no place to stay. I became a street kid, sneaking into places to sleep. But like I said, if you knew how to make the right trade-off, you learned fast enough so that you never had to sleep on the street. After I had been there a few weeks, I met this cute college boy who found me crashing at the Y and told me I could come and stay in his room. He was a really nice guy from New York, and because we had the same size feet, he gave me a pair of his boots. I wore boy boots before it was fashionable. I did it with him a few times, and it was a good place to stay.

Not long after I arrived, I got a job serving food from behind the counter at the cafeteria at the University of Texas, and for a while Austin was a cool place to be. I sat in on classes in history, philosophy, and art. I was in heaven. I wanted to be a student so badly, but obviously this wasn't going to happen. I had a bunch of jobs. I panhandled. I baby-sat. I slept where I could.

The New York guys I met, especially the one I stayed with, were the hippest boys in town, until I actually met the one guy who was one of the hippest guys *in* New York—Lou Reed. It was at a rock club known as the Vulcan Gas Company, where the Velvet Underground was playing. I was clearly not hip, but I'd been there before and I knew the crowd in command of the place—big bossy kids in their twenties who let me into the backstage area. And one night Lou Reed was there, sitting by himself. I was determined to speak to him, and of course I already knew about the Velvet Underground from *Eye* magazine, but no one told me that in New York, and in Andy

Warhol's Factory, people were scared of Lou because he was so hip. The bossy crowd at Vulcan was going, "You can't just go and talk to him, you're not nearly hip enough."

I didn't know Lou Reed had a reputation for reducing people to quivering wrecks with the power of his legendary intellect, but I did know I wasn't going to let these hicks tell me who I couldn't talk to. He was sitting there alone on a folding chair. He didn't seem like any sort of ogre. By the way, I am sure he doesn't remember this happening, because to him it was nothing, but to me it was everything. In fact, once in New York I did say to him, "Do you know I met you in . . . ?" and he brushed me aside. A woman I know who'd been friendly with Lou for a long time got an assignment to do an interview with him. The second she turned on the tape recorder, he became cold, distant, sneering, sarcastic.

When the interview was over, she asked, "Lou, what happened? I thought we were friends."

He said, "Don't you know there are times when I have to be 'Lou Reed'?"

Back to the Vulcan. I'm a Pisces, which means I'm a shoe person, and I fell in love with Lou Reed's boots. I'm like that—you're wearing something cool, I want to talk to you. It doesn't hurt if you're a rock star, but this wasn't premeditated. I just wanted to talk to him because I loved his boots and he was in the Velvet Underground. The first thing I said to him was, "I really like your boots."

He said, "Sit down. Let me tell you a secret."

I could have died and gone to heaven right there and then. And his secret was that they were girls' boots. They were black, and he'd bought them in Denmark, and I said that they were really "groovy" but beyond that I don't remember what I said, only what he said. I really did love his boots, and I suppose he knew I was sincere. And then he pointed to the other people in the room and told me that although they thought they were cool, they were anything but. "They think they're so underground, and they're just FM radio creeps," he added, "and they're not anything." I think he hated everyone there, but he was nice to me. He was like a big brother to me.

Well, I didn't screw Lou Reed. If I had, I'd be happy to tell you that. I could probably say I did, and he wouldn't know the difference. You know, I realize what my reputation in the world probably is, but I wouldn't, then or now, meet somebody and go, "Ooh, I'm gonna sleep with him." Because to me, sleeping with a person isn't that simple. If it were that simple, I might have done it more often. Maybe it's easy for prostitutes, but it's not for regular gals. You don't just have sex, get up, and leave. Guys are on you, they want you, they want to feed you. Right away, they just want to keep you. It's not a situation I jump into willingly.

In Texas I had offers to move in with older guys in their twenties, but I wanted to be free. I thought of going to a commune, but after imagining that I'd have to fuck the cook at the commune to improve my position on the farm, I dropped that idea and fixated on New York City instead. Here was Lou Reed, New

York's finest, talking to me, and that was all I needed to get me going. I was beginning to gain confidence.

After about a year and a half in Austin, I re-established contact with my mother, birthday cards and stuff, with the clear understanding that I was about to hit her up for some money to get to New York. I actually went home to Oklahoma, but my mother and I both knew it was temporary. She really didn't want me back. She was happy with her fourth husband and without any kids around, especially me.

And my stepfather was treating me in the not-very-subtle way a piggish guy treats a sexually aware, possibly sexually active, teenager. When I left two weeks later, Mom was glad to see me go. Eventually, after thirty years of marriage, my stepfather took off with another woman.

What made my mother extra eager to be rid of me was that she could tell I was not quite myself after all the speed I'd been doing in Texas. You see, if you didn't want to screw to get money for food, you just did drugs. Take a little speed, and you can keep moving without having to eat all the time. And everyone had it. The sixties were speed days. I'd been a vagabond in Austin and no longer a cute thing you'd be proud of on the Air Force base. So the plane ticket to New York was fast in coming and a bargain for the whole family. My mother thought it would be better if I was gone, and gone I was.

FOUR
Max's Kansas City

It was the summer of 1971, and I was on a plane to New York City, the most naive, cotton-candy-headed being in the world. No fear, no expectations of danger or of being hurt. The only fear I'd experienced was at home. In my mind I was going to be safe anyplace but home.

I had a Samsonite suitcase, a little travel bag, about $300, and, I thought, a reservation at the Barbizon Hotel for women, which my mother was supposed to have made. But she hadn't. She just sent me away. I had a lot of clothes on, which I thought was proper—a habit I soon learned to abandon. Lots of layers, stockings, what I thought was a very mod pair of shoes, a skirt and blouse, and many undergarments. A proper Southern outfit couldn't have been more wrong for New York.

The Barbizon had no room for me and suggested the 36th Street Y, which is where I ended up for $30 a week. A hotbed of lesbianism, but I didn't care; I was in New York. Girls would follow me around from the minute I checked in. I'd been on my own for a year, and I was used to people chasing me around. Girls, boys, what's the difference? It's all the same trip; they all want something. The Y was neat and clean, and I practically had my own bathroom; I had to share it with only one other girl. I tried to get a job and interviewed at these places where they gave me typing tests, which I failed immediately and consistently.

In 1971 New York was so radically different from what it is today that I'm going to have to ask you to really stretch your imagination. Try this: Twenty-five years back from *that* date was 1946! Men wore fedoras all day long, women had those big, heavy hairdos, there was no TV or air conditioning, music was "the big band sound," and practically no one had been born yet, except I think Charlie Watts.

Well, there I was, looking around at real New Yorkers, and I knew that I didn't belong. At the age of nineteen, you were supposed to be truly swinging, and I was so unhip. But people were nice. The lesbians were always leaving little gifts outside my door, the woman at the downstairs desk tried to find me jobs, and the elderly black man who ran the elevator rescued me when the dykes were pressing in too close. Old men were always going, "Say there, Miss," because I looked like an easy pickup, and I would stand there and actually talk to them. Or I'd meet someone for dinner and all of a sudden a hand would be groping under the table and the mouth would be saying, "Oh, have another drink!" "Sorry, I've gotta go now," I'd say. I was used to escaping. That part wasn't difficult.

Thinking about it now, I was very lucky. God or whoever was really watching over me. You know, those guys I hitchhiked to Texas with could have been murderers, and I could have been undone in a thousand ways. But something protects me—a little bit of bullshit, a little bit of creativity, and instincts kick in—not always in the nick of time, as I'd find out with Steven Tyler, but in enough time to keep me from going over the edge.

I mean, how many people arrived in Manhattan for the first time on the same day I did? How many gave it a shot and lasted? Who got killed, or used, or abused? Who turned into a prostitute, or decided to be normal and go home and marry their childhood sweetheart? Who died of AIDS or in the gutter? Who got really rich and successful and can hide the stories about an abused childhood and would not dream of writing a tell-all book? And then there's me, and my friends from those days, battered but still here, having traveled all over the world but still living in New York. My darling friend Lillian Roxon, who wrote *The Rock Encyclopedia* and died in 1974, used to say that if you told her she could never leave New York, she might consider killing herself, but if you told her she would have to leave and never come back, she would kill herself without hesitation.

One of the first things I did when I got to New York was change my name from Kathleen Victoria to Cyrinda. When I was very young, I'd known a girl

named Cyrinda, and I always knew I'd use that name
someday. It was also very close to my big sister's
name, Lynda. And I changed my looks as well. Gone
were the proper Southern shoes and layers, and in
came very 1940s platform heels, rolled-up jeans with
seamed stockings, and those tiny little velvet tops. I
started bleaching my hair, because in case you
haven't guessed, I am not a natural blonde. I even
bleached my pubic hair to match the hair on my head.
When I started getting wilder and more stylish, I
shaved my pubic hair into the shape of a heart. I must
have been on speed when I did that, because it's not
something one could accomplish casually. It's a speed
kind of thing, like the people who paper the walls of
their homes with penny postage stamps, one at a time.

The clubs in New York that I'd read about were
the Cheetah, the Hippodrome, and Steve Paul's The
Scene, and I figured that's where I'd find people my
own age who were free. I had this fantasy about some
dream place where everyone would be cool and fabulous, and I found that it actually existed. It was
called Max's Kansas City. I got taken there by a hippie girl from the Y who was on her way out one night
and asked if I wanted to go with her. So I put on one
of my vintage outfits that looked like leaves, with a
little slip underneath, and off we went to some strange
neighborhood way off the beaten track. Suddenly I
was in front of the place that was going to be the
center of my life for the next few years—Max's Kansas City—my world, nearly complete unto itself.

If you don't know about Max's, it was a restaurant

that served lunch to insurance executives during the
day, because it was in a dreary insurance neighborhood on Park Avenue South just north of Union
Square. At night it became the hangout for all of the
most creative people in New York, London, and beyond. A lot of that had to do with Mickey Ruskin,
who besides Max's owned extremely hip clubs on the
Lower East Side and in the Village, and who had a
crowd of artists and poets and photographers that
would hang out at whatever club he opened. Andy
Warhol had moved his studio, known as the Factory,
to Max's neighborhood around 1967, and so all his
people were there. That meant lots of drag queens,
along with tough, brilliant women such as Brigid Polk
and Viva, and then of course the fags. Later Max's
became a hangout for the rock stars such as Janis
Joplin, the Grateful Dead, and the Doors, who stayed
at the Chelsea Hotel.

When the artsy Harvard Square people moved to
New York, they went to Max's. When people like
Germaine Greer visited New York from London, they
went to Max's. The Kennedys, the Stones, Bob Dy-
lan, and the Cockettes all went there. Anyone fabulous who came to New York from Australia got taken
to Max's by Lillian Roxon. Jim Morrison peed into
an empty wine bottle at Max's, put the cork back in,
told the waitress that he couldn't finish his wine, and
suggested that she take it home. She was thrilled.

You never needed any money at Max's. If Mickey
knew you, you could sit there all night and help yourself to coffee, or sign the check and never hear about

it again. Some of Mickey's heavy drinking buddies, the crowd that we called the Abstract Expressionist Heterosexual Alcoholics, ran up tabs of $60,000 and $70,000, and this was a place where a steak dinner was less than $5. But those people sat at tables in the front where the bar was located. Upstairs there was a disco where Wayne County (now Jayne County) played records and the different Max's "elements" came together. There was no disco music per se back then; people danced to rock and roll, and at the end of every night Wayne ended the program with "Gimme Shelter," a nice, apocalyptic finish for a crowd that had danced enough for one night.

My friends, the Warhols, the queers, and the musicians, hung out in the Back Room, a unique little universe in and of itself past all the tables, the phone booths, and the restrooms. It was just a room with tables, including a big round one in the right-hand corner and booths lining the walls. It was Action Central of the entire New York underground scene from the time Max's opened in 1965 until it closed about ten years after I got to town.

The thing about Max's was that it was never in the columns and wasn't famous in the way that Studio 54 and other places that followed were famous. You either knew about it or you didn't. It was so off the beaten path that no one was likely to stumble in. And if you did and looked particularly dorky, one look from Dorothy Dean, who was seated on a stool near the cash register at the door, told you that you'd made a mistake. There was no security, no velvet ropes, no bouncers with biceps, only Dorothy Dean, a size two black woman with glasses, who was universally acknowledged as the most terrifying and brilliant person in New York.

A graduate of Radcliffe, Dorothy—who died about ten years ago of cancer in Boulder, Colorado—is now the darling of cultural historians of that era. There was a story about her in the *New Yorker*, and the headline read something like READ ALL ABOUT THE BLACK CLIFFIE WHO RULED NEW YORK'S GAY SOCIETY! She was brilliant and fearless. She could scare policemen, politicians, celebrities, and the meanest queens in town. And on my first trip there, she was really nice to me. I had wandered into the Back Room, and she sat down and we talked. Like Lou Reed, I think it was about shoes. I learned later that she had a reputation for cherishing gorgeous, expensive shoes, but anyhow, the sight of Dorothy talking to a newcomer carried a lot of weight, and in the course of my first visit to Max's, I was in. This was not a dykey move on her part. Dorothy had a wild sex life, but it was all boys and men, especially boys.

So there I was in the Back Room, chatting with Dorothy Dean and checking out what people were wearing. The person I was most taken with was this tall woman in a black slip dress and high heels. She was the most beautiful and glamorous woman I'd ever seen. Her name was Candy Darling, né James Slattery, and she seemed perfect, wearing the most exquisite makeup, with platinum hair and milky-white skin.

Thus my first two human encounters (if you count staring at Candy Darling as an encounter) at Max's were with maximum icons of the gay universe. And then there was Leee Childers, who came over to me that same evening and said, "We are interested in you." He soon became, and still is, my best friend. To this day, Leee still can't believe that Dorothy Dean was so nice to me my first time at Max's, and admits that he was so impressed that he decided to find out who I was and what I was about. Naturally, the feeling was mutual.

According to *Robert Mapplethorpe: A Biography* by Patricia Morrisroe, Robert Mapplethorpe and Patti Smith stood in the doorway to the Back Room night after night for months, wanting to be part of it. As it turned out, everyone was wondering who they were, because they were awfully intriguing in their black leather as potential sex objects for the Back Room crowd, Robert especially. Here are two people who went on to become world famous, and they spent months being terrified about being rejected by the Back Room crowd. Finally some queen said to them, "Why don't you sit down here?" and that's how they broke in.

I remember seeing Patti Smith for the first time and asking, "Who's that guy?" Mapplethorpe was a precious little thing, but I thought he was totally unhip. And his photos don't interest me, he didn't interest me, and he'd just look at me as if I totally didn't interest him. I was impressed when Patti became a college-age icon. I was never a big fan of hers, but I was happy that a Back Room person was making it big.

I had been absorbed and adopted on the spot by the cream of the New York gay underground, even though they treated me like a baby. "We're going to take a walk in the Village now," they'd say, and they'd fight over whether I could come along, but it was all a game. They were acting out some code. You see, I was bait. I was told, "If any guys come up and talk to us, you just talk to them for a few minutes, and then we'll take over." These were fags and drag queens; a real girl was just what they needed to soften the prey up before they started weaving their web. Not that it was in any way sinister. I mean, they never kidnapped children and brought them to orgies or torture chambers. And what a crowd it was—Leee, Candy, Andy Warhol, Jackie Curtis, Holly Woodlawn, everyone around me was gay, vibrant, creative, eccentric, intelligent. They were the ultimate males for me, and I could be their ultimate female.

Even though I was shy and didn't talk much at the beginning, they would dress me up, parade me around, and use me to attract straight guys. I thought it was all divine. They introduced me to this really beautiful boy; he looked like Jackson Browne, but he was very gay, very effeminate. He wore these peasant blouses embroidered with sunflowers, and he was just gorgeous. And he, along with Leee and all the rest, began my makeover.

They gave me black lips, because they said in the old black-and-white movies they used black lipstick.

I had never smoked a cigarette, so my teeth were like pearls. I plucked out my eyebrows and drew in these high arches. So, with my raccoon eyes and platinum hair (it took them two whole days to strip it to pure platinum), and wild, glamorous clothing—like electric-colored, skin-tight fifties dresses—I was made.

It was that look which attracted the attention of Andy Warhol and his people. I mean, you show up at Gloria Vanderbilt's for dinner with Christie Brinkley on your arm and everyone says, "Oh, what a pretty girl!" But you show up with Cyrinda and they go, "Oh my God, what is that?" And, of course, that's what Andy wanted. He wanted to be surrounded by both the beautiful and the bizarre.

My movie debut, however, had nothing to do with Andy and everything to do with, of all people, John Lennon and Yoko Ono. They had moved to New York a couple of years earlier and were pulling out all the stops to establish themselves as bona fide members of New York's avant-garde. It was said that Yoko was trying to be on the edge of the edge in her earlier days in New York but wasn't having much success. So she went and married John Lennon, and when they arrived, there was no stopping them. They could do whatever they wanted, and the world had to stop and pay attention. It was her revenge on the crowd that didn't totally accept her in the first place.

John and Yoko were making a short film called *Legs*, which was just hundreds of photos of people's legs shot on video. They had a photo of Virginia Lust with flies all over her legs—all terribly trendy. I was a little nobody, just a body with a pair of legs. I had this bronze frog glued to my chest, I'm not sure why, which John Lennon appeared to be very interested in (the frog, that is; my chest wasn't very interesting, even then). He talked to me a lot, and I actually got paid with a dollar bill autographed by him. I went to Max's later that night and spent it, though people told me I should save it for its value as a collectible.

I met John Lennon a few more times after that, because he was really good friends with Bob Gruen, who was the "official" photographer of practically everything, mainly the Lennons, the Dolls, and *Rock Scene* magazine. John was funny and really kind, but it was hard for me to make the connection back to when I was twelve and Beatlemania was in full swing, because to me he just looked like this older guy who was kind of eccentric.

Leee Childers was pivotal to me in those early years. I loved his cultivated, silky Kentucky upper-class accent, and he had beautiful blue eyes. He was a photographer, and he started taking pictures of me. I wasn't anyone important, but he treated me as if I were the most precious thing he'd ever found. When I asked about that beautiful "woman," Candy Darling, I became extra precious, because to him my naiveté meant I could be molded into a most compliant companion. It amused him to have a new toy, and I was cute—for a girl.

Oh, Candy. She was the greatest and always the most beautiful. At first she didn't like me being around. Here's this young blond girl with platinum hair and black lipstick, and I was sort of copying her look. Once I was at a party with these two guys, waiting for the elevator, and Candy got off and looked me up and down, and one of these wiseass guys smirked and said, "I wonder which one is the real Candy Darling."

And I shot back, "The one with the cock between his legs." I was learning that you can't let people roll over you, not in New York City. Answering back is like putting up a hand and blocking a hit. After that, Candy and I became really good friends, like sisters. I loved Candy until the day she died. She was the closest thing to the grooviest woman I've ever known. She'd tell me about men and warn me: no drinking (it makes the muscles in your face fall), no drugs, and no smoking, ever, because it smells bad and turns you ugly colors in the wrong places. And she said you really never should have sex with men if you can avoid it. She didn't like sex very much, and she'd tell me, "You're a beautiful woman. You don't have to do that unless you really want to, because they just want to use you and own you." How true that turned out to be.

We had this thing where I would check out Candy from the bottom of a staircase to make sure her cock was tucked away just right so it looked like a girl's crotch. I thought it looked uncomfortable, but she assured me, "No, no, it's not." And she took hormone pills by the handful to make her breasts grow. To this day people think that the hormones gave her cancer.

Back to Leee and my early training period: We'd

go back to his place and watch old movies. It was there that he turned me on to Marlene Dietrich. He'd take me to thrift shops where they had these beautiful, inexpensive clothes from the twenties, thirties, and forties. Life was no longer normal. It was what I had always wanted. You couldn't just go to Bloomingdale's and buy a dress, you had to do something different. Oh, when Leee told me, "We are interested in you" that first night at Max's, there was more to it. His crowd was doing a play called *Pork*, and they wanted me to be in it. My brief life on the wicked stage was about to begin.

FIVE
Miss Piggy Stardust

Pork was created by Andy Warhol and Brigid Polk. Brigid, née Brigid Berlin, was and still is one of this century's most amazing people. The daughter of the president of the Hearst Corporation, she grew up on Fifth Avenue, with the Duke and Duchess of Windsor and J. Edgar Hoover as her family's best friends.

Brigid rebelled at an early age, spent a trust fund of several hundred thousand dollars one summer at the gay enclave of Cherry Grove on Fire Island, and became an infamous speed freak. She was also Andy's best friend, photographed everything with her Polaroid camera, and taped every phone call she ever made. She's a fabulous artist, too. She uses her nipples instead of brushes. Known as "Tit Prints," her works are still exhibited. There was a show of them in spring of 1996 at the chic Jane Stubbs New York gallery. She's still wildly talented but like many of us is now antidrugs.

Brigid and Andy had turned a bunch of her phone call transcripts into a play called *Pork*, and it was

performed by a crowd of Back Room theater people.
It was Andy's first contact with the exploding world
of New York underground theater (except for using
all the drag queen stars in his movies), and the alli-
ance was not exactly seamless. Nevertheless, there I
was, barely off the boat from serving cafeteria food
at the University of Texas at Austin, and I was being
asked to be an off-off-Broadway star. They weren't
exactly offering me a starring role, but I was determined that a star was what I was going to be. In all
modesty, there really wasn't a pre-existing role for
me in *Pork*, but I was so fabulous looking that the
director, Tony Ingrassia, told Leee that he had to have
me in the show. Andy had taken a step back once
he'd handed the play over to Tony, and told him to
use a bunch of new people in the cast. So they invented a part for me as the nonspeaking lesbian side-
kick of a genuine lunatic named Via Valentina. I
don't remember what my character's name was. Also
in the cast were Gerri Miller, Cherry Vanilla, and
Harvey Fierstein, who was unknown then and would
later gain fame for his play *Torch Song Trilogy*.

There were no drag queens in this production,
which was *not* the way Andy's movies directed by
Paul Morrissey were cast. I didn't know it at the time,
but it had become a political thing, and all the old
drag queens were getting pushed out of the Warhol
circle. Paul still wanted them around, but Andy didn't
want anything to do with them. When they were cast-
ing the movie *Heat*, Andy wanted me in it, but Paul
insisted, "No, it's not her time." and Andy said,

"What are you talking about?" and they were yelling, really yelling at each other in the front room of the Factory on Union Square North. I'd never seen Andy so pissed off. Right around this time, Paul and Andy ended their business partnership, so it was a pivotal point in Andy's career.

In *Pork*, I was supposed to sit around in red clothes, platform heels, and black lips and squeeze lightbulbs, and they would light up in my hands. I loved it. I'd find someone in the audience who was watching me, and I'd play right to him or her for all it was worth. I didn't have any lines, and one night I got so tired of not being able to speak, because I was getting all this attention and the press had started writing about my "style," so I decided to talk. I just threw in a line or two that wasn't in the script, and I got a laugh from the audience. The bug had bit, I had it, I wanted it, I wanted to be on stage every night, in a theater with an audience.

As you might imagine, improvising lines where there are none is a very uncool thing to do. I was almost beaten by the director and the other cast members. Tony Zanetta, who played Andy Warhol, was screaming, "How dare she?" He wanted me out of the play immediately. So I said, "Well, I'll just leave," but they knew I was getting a lot of notice and they had to ask me to stay. It was like being in a B movie. Ha ha, the fags got hold of me and then tried to hold me down, but I was getting too slippery even for them, and I had Andy on my side. And I was getting great reviews, you know, "Who is this blonde? Could there be a real woman back in the Warhol stable?" Which wasn't fair to Cherry and Gerri; they were real women, God knows.

It was at a rehearsal for *Pork* that I first saw Andy. I didn't even know who he was. "Who's that funny little old man with the silver wig?" I asked, and they all laughed at me. Who, indeed!

I was very naive, and here was this cute little guy, and it was Andy Warhol, and everyone is going, "Oh, darling, you really don't know anything, do you? That's the man you're working for!"

I think Andy thought it was adorable that I didn't know who he was, or at least didn't recognize him, because of course I knew his name, but I really didn't know what he looked like. I think I'd seen him once on the news, maybe. What the hell did I know?

I don't care what they say about Andy, he was a very tender guy. I will never, ever say a bad thing about Andy. He was charming, and I do think he liked women very much—he did only good things for me, though I can't pretend not to have heard others complain about not getting paid and so forth. That's crap. He did good things for everyone around him. He opened doors for people who couldn't have opened them on their own. He had a brilliant and courageous mind, and he was always experimenting. If you were lucky enough to be a part of this magical man's trip, the doors did fly open. I've never known anyone like him in my life, or seen anything like him, either.

After I got the part in the play, he brought me into his circle, and we would talk about dopey things, like being Catholic and what we liked about going to church, because he was very Catholic, and his mother lived with him until she died at a very old age, and she was super-devout. I think Andy was a very caring person, but he cultivated this cool front, as if he cared about nothing at all. "Oh, that's nice," he'd say. "Oh, fabulous." "Oh."

He was the first person I knew who saw everything and missed nothing. He was meticulous about details and not great company in a crowd. He didn't have to be, he just had to be there, and all eyes were on him. But when you were alone with him, he was a real chatterbox. He reminded me of Merv Griffin in a lot of ways. They had common mannerisms and both said, "Oooh," all the time.

Andy always wanted to fix me up with "really great" guys, and I would just say, "No way," and it made him crazy that I wouldn't follow his advice about men. These European movie stars would come to town and he wanted me to date them, but I wouldn't do it. I didn't like to be told what to do. I suppose it was good advice, but it wasn't what I wanted. I didn't want someone controlling my life, even if it was Andy Warhol. In other areas of my life, I did listen to Andy, and I must say I did learn a lot— about getting facials regularly, going to the right stores and art galleries, and saying hello to this person and that person. *Fine.* But dating these heirs with an eye to marriage, no, no, no.

Andy did my portrait, and I went to beautiful restaurants and beautiful places with him, and he was so nice and tried so hard to help me, but this whole thing about dating rich men and climbing in society was just what I did not want to hear. I did not want to conform. I wanted to be wild and free and stay up and dance with fags all night long if I felt like it, and that would have ended immediately if I had to start going out with these real rich men in their $2000 suits (that was a lot of money for a suit back then). I would have had to start changing my clothes, those kinky little dresses would be gone, and I'd have been wearing sensible little frocks and having children at age twenty. I didn't want to be some rich guy's toy, and the Warhol crowd was trying to get me into that. "You should go with him, you should sleep with him, you should try to marry him," they'd say. It was like they were pimping me while they, the Warhol crowd, climbed into higher and more conservative social circles and tried to shed their downtown, gay, druggy roots. I'd rather be used by my Lower East Side fags to attract a cute guy for *them* to sleep with than be used by the Warhol circle to attract someone rich and international into *their* circle.

In retrospect, it seems ironic that Andy and the crowd who practically invented the underground in New York in the sixties were becoming so conservative and socialite with such a vengeance in the seventies. It makes sense, though, because Andy was always ahead of his time. But for me, I wanted to enjoy the seventies. I wanted to be in that moment, when everything was so extravagant and creative and self-expressive.

I had a great time with Andy and I always loved him. He died on my birthday in 1987, right before I returned to New York, and it was very sad. There were many people affected by his death, because he was *the* Andy Warhol, a whole universe in and of himself. When he died, that whole thing he invented, that whole kind of crazy fame and eccentric glamour, just fell out of New York City forever. Nothing has ever taken its place. His collections were auctioned off, and then there were occasional parties at the Gershwin Hotel for those who survived and remember how special it was being a Warhol person.

While Andy was trying to fix me up with Euro-guys, I was loving my downtown queers more than ever. All those fags were much more to my liking than "real" men. I knew they had sex with each other, but that wasn't a big deal to me. They made me look like the ultimate sex symbol of our world—New York underground pop culture. I was the Marilyn of our scene. It was all dressing up and playing dress-up. I didn't even date anyone. Leee Childers to this day says to me, "You looked like the biggest fuck me babe in town, but you hardly fucked anybody."

I knew the queens were doing drugs, but I wasn't asked to share them. No one ever offered me even one tiny morsel of those drugs, not even Jackie Curtis with all her speed. Jackie was a playwright, an actress, a singer, a partial drag queen, always in need of a shave, and a speed addict, although she later died of a heroin overdose. She always smelled a little rancid, wore glitter and torn stockings, and was, in every way, *Too Much*. Her grandmother was Slugger Ann, a legendary bar owner on Second Avenue.

I thought these people were simply divine lunatics, wild, crazy, and wonderful. There was a lot of drinking, but I just drank ginger ale. I didn't like alcohol. It was, for me, renaissance time, surrounded by people who were so creative with themselves. I didn't eat very much; everyone else who was on speed hardly ate at all. Some fruit and a container of yogurt would do me for the whole day.

I had to do something for a living. I had a job for a little while in a dress shop or something, but not for long. I was an artist at Nina Needlepoint's up on Madison Avenue where I painted fabrics. That was fun. As for sex, the only person I remember screwing back then was Rita Red, a sweet, gentle gay man whose real name was Richie Zollo.

During those days I felt much more comfortable with homosexuals than with straight guys. Fags were more fun. I was constantly delighted, mesmerized, and fascinated. They were still guys, and that's one interesting thing people forget. I don't care if a man is wearing a dress, he's still a guy in a dress. I don't care if he thinks he's a woman, because he isn't. Even gay men carry certain attitudes and reactions that remain male, and all of that appealed to me, because I like males, no matter who *they* like.

Girls were a problem when it came to making friends. There was Via Valentina, who was in *Pork*, and she became a friend of mine, but for some odd reason she liked to hit me and I just hated that. She'd hit me so hard I would get these bruises on my arms. Gerri Miller, who was also in *Pork*, became a friend, too. She had these huge tits and would dance in strip joints. She was highly sought after because she would put tassels on her nipples and twirl them in opposite directions at once. She was a real sweetheart, but sadly, I heard she's now down and out.

Other gal pals during that time included female beauties Jane Forth and Donna Jordan, as well as Lillian Roxon, who was very dear. Lillian once did a story on the scene at Max's for an Australian newspaper. The article was all about the local freaks and when Leee complained to her that I wasn't in it, Lillian said, "Cyrinda is not a freak. She's a dear, beautiful, innocent girl. I am sorry to deny her publicity, but she does not belong in this list." I adored Lillian. I think she worried about me a little bit. She always wanted to know how I was doing and what was going on. She knew I was hanging out with a rough, self-destructive group, and she knew the scene better than I did. I thought it was just putting on sequins, but she knew better. These people were playing with fire. When they weren't getting the attention they thought they deserved, they were dangerous. Like that nothing, Valerie Solanis, the man-hater, who shot Andy Warhol in 1968.

Somehow I muddled through without getting terribly hurt. I was living on Ninth Street between First and A, in Penny Arcade's apartment. I hadn't known Penny, but she was a famous underground star. She'd gone to Amsterdam, and a mutual friend got me to move in and house sit, which I did, and pay the rent, which I'm afraid I didn't. Four hundred and fifty dollars a month was out of the question, especially with my fashion budget. I'm afraid I was not a responsible person. I think Penny hates me to this day, because when she was in Amsterdam she heard that she was getting evicted. She flew back to New York, let herself in the apartment, and found me naked and lying on the floor with my wrists cut. This was only one of my dozen or so drama-queen suicide attempts, which was the thing back then.

Penny doesn't take any bullshit, and she was not pleased. She walked over and sort of nudged me, not all that gently, with her foot. I came out of my unsuccessful suicidal stupor at that point, sat up, and asked this complete stranger what time it was. When she told me, I said, "Oh my God, I have to be at Max's," and I ran to the bathroom, bandaged my wrists, and was out the door. Penny threw me out of her house the next day and wrote a song about the experience.

Steven Piven was one who was successful in his suicide attempt. He was this incredibly beautiful blond boy around twenty with whom all the fags were in love. It took your breath away just to look at him. He also had a small part in *Pork*, and his apartment was next door to Penny's apartment. He took a bunch of pills and died there. Now this boy was so beautiful that people were afraid to approach him, or even to call him on the phone, because everyone thought that he would think you were coming on to him. Why else would you talk to a person who was so good-looking? It was uncool to make the first move with Steven Piven, even just a social one. You were supposed to wait until he called you. Turns out no one ever called him, and he was so depressed that he killed himself.

Unfortunately, his body wasn't discovered right away and started decomposing. After ten days the stench was unbearable. It took over my whole apartment, and I couldn't tell where it was coming from. There was a hole in the wall between his apartment and mine, and Penny's little kittens were going crazy from the smell and scratching me all the time. In fact, all the people and animals in the building were going cuckoo. There were maggots falling from Steven's apartment into the apartment beneath his, and I think everyone was in denial that there was a death in the building.

Finally, these Polish people who lived on the other side of Steven called the police, who broke down the door. Millions of huge flies swarmed out, and when I looked in I saw that Steven had turned into this big black thing lying on the floor, ready to explode. I'd never even been to a funeral. The closest I'd been to death was seeing those warehouses full of caskets in the Philippines, and I fainted right there in the hall.

He'd written a note to me saying he was sorry, and next to his body was his portfolio, all covered with death bugs, and it featured a full-page fashion ad from the *New York Times* in which he was the model. The authorities had him buried in a hurry, and by the time his family was notified, he was six feet under, and they refused to believe it. His two brothers and a girl came to my apartment and started screaming at me that it wasn't him. They were in a frenzy, because they had exhumed the body and it was not his height or something, and they were calling me a liar for telling the police that it was Steven. They went on screaming and accusing me of some kind of hoax, and I said, "Look, kids, I know that was him, and the only way I know is because of the shirt he was wearing, a tie-dyed blue shirt that I knew was his, because the rest of him was not recognizable." We actually stood there fighting about this poor dead guy who was their brother.

On to happier memories! This was the year I was traveling through all these levels of New York party society because of all the pictures of me in the magazines of my "silent" part in *Pork*. I met Warren Beatty, Cecil Beaton, the von Furstenbergs, and then, through my boss, Sam Green, I met Greta Garbo. In fact, Sam introduced me to many famous people who were his intimate friends. If you read the book *Savage Grace*, it's all about Sam, because he was extremely close to Barbara Bakeland, the Bakelite heiress, and her son Tony, who murdered her and then killed himself in jail by putting a plastic (!!) bag over his head. Everyone says that Barbara and her son were sleeping together and that they were both in love with Sam. He's very modest about the whole thing, but they were at his house a lot, and he'd leave me alone with Tony all the time, who I must say was a bit strange.

A famous international art dealer and consultant,

Sam Green needed someone like me who gave good phone, so every morning I'd dress up, go to his house off Central Park West, and be divine on the phone. One morning this woman called and asked for Sam. She said she was Miss Brown. I told Sam that Miss Brown was calling, and he said, "Oh, I'll take that." He later told me it was Greta Garbo. They were good friends, and she always identified herself as Miss Brown. She called every morning at eight-thirty, and talked for an hour. Andy Warhol would call at about nine-thirty, and then *they'd* talk for an hour. So Sam needed someone to handle the phones when he was doing his daily catchups with Andy and Miss Brown.

Sometimes Garbo would come over to Sam's house. He told me just to talk about simple things, and never ask her questions about her career in movies. Also I was instructed not to refer to her as Miss Garbo or tell her that someone said to say hello, because if I did she'd know I was talking about her to someone else.

The first time I met Garbo, I had to bring some packages over to her house. On my way up in the elevator I ran into Rex Harrison, who lived in the same building, and I swear to God he tried to pick me up. Amazed as I was, I turned the offer down and went to Garbo's apartment, where she offered me a vodka. It was really early in the morning, and she was wearing slacks and a sweater and was barefoot. I didn't notice that she had Flintstone feet like the legend says, but she was thin and had great bones, and her skin looked tired.

Once, she was going to walk home through Central Park from Sam's house to her apartment on East 52nd Street, and Sam asked me to go with her. She walked fast, kept her head down, and was not recognized the whole time. "Don't look at people," she said to me as we clipped along. Once or twice, we'd sit on a bench and rest for a few minutes. I was the one who needed to rest, not her. She could really move along, and I had on high on heels. She was easy to talk to about really trivial things—squirrels, the trees, the weather, if we should go up that hill or around it—and to me she was just this nice, elderly woman who knew what she wanted, which was not to be bothered. She gave me good womanly advice: Everyone sucks, and privacy is the most important thing. She was neither affectionate nor cold. Little me and one of the world's Ultimate Women. I'll never forget it, and you can bet I was becoming spoiled.

Another friend of Sam's whom I spent some time with was Marcel Duchamp, the French artist who led the Dada movement. You know, his "art" was a urinal on a pedestal. I had no idea he was one of the seminal figures of twentieth-century art. To me he was just a sweet old guy who had a very courtly European manner. Sam told me he knew that charming, brilliant, talented old geniuses would find me "delightful," because I was pretty, well-dressed, well-mannered, and sexy, and reminded him of Marilyn Monroe in *The Prince and the Showgirl*. I think that's one of the nicest compliments I've ever received. Cecil Beaton told Sam he thought I was prettier than Marilyn, and

Sam insisted I repeat that in this book, but I blush a bit to do so.

I want to make sure everyone knows I met Tennessee Williams, even though he was out-of-his-mind drunk at the time (it was at Andy's Factory). It's impressive—to me, anyhow—to be able to say I met such a great genius. I'm not sure you could tell what a genius he was at the time, but his works speak for themselves, don't they?

And Keith Richards, my great idol. I met him at a friend's house. I walked right up to him and told him he was the coolest musician of them all. He was just wonderful about it; gracious and funny, not in a pretentious, phony way like other famous people. It's said that he has one of the best marriages in all rock and roll and that everybody loves his wife, Patti. Good. He deserves that.

I'll take music, knowledge, friends, respect, love, and money gratefully, but fame I didn't chase, and I don't regret it. I chased people who were already famous, or, as I would prefer to think, they chased me. I even got chased by Ike Turner! When I was hanging out with Jackie Curtis and Leee Childers, somebody said there was a big party being given by Ike and Tina Turner at the St. Regis. No one had an invitation, and I guess I looked the most welcomable, dressed as I was in a skin-tight red dress with my platinum blond hair. My friends stuck me in front of all of them, and I knocked on the door of Ike and Tina's suite. When the door opened there were about a dozen black body-guards standing there, and I said, "Hi." One of the guards said to me, "Well, you can come in if you give me a kiss," and I did. A second later I blurted, "And these are my friends!" and this little crowd trooped in behind me.

So we're sitting around the dining room table, me, Leee, and Jackie, and everyone is very nice, and there are these dinner-sized plates piled with cocaine going around the room. All my friends are bindling it up and packing it away, and all of a sudden this big black hand is on my arm and a guy says, "I think you better come over here."

He takes me into the kitchen where Ike is sitting on a little sink. And Ike says, "Why don't you stay a while?"

And I say, "I really have to go home, because I just remembered that I left all the burners on my stove lit to heat up the apartment and maybe it's dangerous."

So he says, "I'll tell you what. I'll have someone take you home so you can turn them off, and then you come back, okay?"

And I'm going, "I really don't think so," and I got out of there.

Marian Javits, the wild wife of the U.S. senator from New York, was another problem. I met her at a party at Sam's, and I think she was drunk. She was getting very close to me and just not shutting up, when some people came over and literally picked her up and carried her away! I'd never seen anything like it. They lifted her up in the air and carried her across the room and put her down somewhere else. "We just saved you from a fate worse than death," one of my rescuers told me.

Al Pacino was a stinky nuisance. He was the janitor in Sam's building and slept on this filthy mattress under the staircase. He was grubby, disgusting, smelly, and drunk, and he used to look up my skirt when I went up the stairs. There was nothing appealing about him at all. He was an aspiring actor but too soused to get any work. According to legend, Lee Strasberg of the Actor's Studio spotted him at a party and told him that if he cleaned up his act, he'd let him study at the Studio. And that's what happened!

Candy Darling, my wonderful friend, was very close to Salvador and Gala Dali, and we used to meet up with them at funky bars. One time I was sitting next to Gala, and in the midst of our casual conversation I felt her hand on my knee, and then it started to slide up my thigh. I wondered at first if this was some European custom, but I soon got nervous and excused myself. On the way to the ladies' room I gave Candy a little "help!" signal and she followed me in. I asked, "Is she just being friendly?" and Candy said, "Oh, honey, no. Keep your legs close together when you sit next to her."

My eyes were opening. I was where I wanted to be. Nobody was telling me what to do. I was high on life. You could go and be in a play for a night or a week. Off-off-Broadway was in its heyday. Then you'd go to Max's and dance until four in the morning, showing off for photographers and artists. Jane

Fonda would show up with Roger Vadim. Downtown was really alive, especially around Macdougal Street, where there were lots of music clubs and bars.

What's more, I was going to museums and gallery openings and parties in penthouses and movie screenings and all this kind of uptown stuff, which was beginning to feel a little unnatural. This was with Sam Green and the Warhol people, because they were social climbing at twice the speed of light. All that was very wonderful, especially going to museums and looking at paintings I'd seen only in pictures. But cool as it was, my heart was downtown at Max's on Avenue A. Where was the rock and roll that had been so important earlier? It was happening in New York, soon to be revealed to me in the form of the New York Dolls, the hottest group in town, whose lead singer I married in 1977. It was also coming from England, in the person of the hottest new star in the world, David Bowie, soon to be my first big-time rock-and-roll lover.

At the end of 1971, *Pork* went to London without me. I had had terrible fights with the director and lead actor because I spoke on stage in my nonspeaking role. But I was having a great time doing the town with the Warhol crowd and was planning to do another play with Jackie Curtis. The bottom line is, I stayed behind. Actually, I was afraid to go to England with them. I felt safer in New York.

Bear in mind that *Pork* was a play supposedly by and about Andy Warhol, so it was a sensation in the hippest circles of the London underground. And, of course, no one was watching the trends in American art, music, and fashion more closely than David Bowie, who was just beginning to make a name for himself in Britain as a sensational, androgynous new-comer. He wore a dress and was very pretty, and everyone thought he was gay, which he encouraged because it was a good gimmick.

David had a knack for spotting the most revolu-tionary talents around. Some people say that's always been his greatest talent, but I happen to think he's a super musician as well, and if he's been, shall we say, influenced by others, he's picked good people from whom to learn. He was an early fan of the Velvet Underground and noticed Iggy Pop long before prac-tically anyone in America did. Bowie and his people glommed onto the *Pork* people in a big way. Bowie's manager, Tony DeFries, was the director of a com-pany called Main Man. He was fast-talking, faintly sleazy, definitely not one of "us," but he had an im-mense and unlimited amount of money to spend and was eager to use this money to send word back to New York with the *Pork* crowd of the imminent ar-rival of the great English rock star, David Bowie.

And so Leee, Wayne County, Tony Zanetta, and Cherry Vanilla all came back from London as *em-ployees* of Main Man. They had so much money to spend that after the late, great Bob Feiden saw them in action, he coined the term *expensive account*. They came to Max's in limousines, rented new apartments on gorgeous streets in Chelsea, ordered champagne for everyone, bought themselves color TVs, had their

teeth capped, you name it. For a while, it seemed as
if everyone in the Back Room at Max's was being
subsidized by Main Man. *You're spreading goodwill
for David Bowie? Fine, I'll have a magnum of Veuve
Cliquot, if you promise to think very highly and often
of David.* It was unbelievable. People who couldn't
pay the rent on their squalid flats a few months before
were now spending thousands a week on frivolities,
setting up Main Man's New York office, and sending
the bills to Mr. DeFries.

No one knew where the DeFries dollars came from.
It was obvious when you met him that he was not
born with a silver spoon in his mouth. I'd learned
from Andy how to spot the mannerisms that accom-
pany inherited wealth, but you didn't need a teacher
to know that the DeFries family was not prominent
in Burke's Peerage. There were rumors that he traded
fast and loose on the gold market, which was a sat-
isfying explanation for all that cash.

"You've *got* to meet David Bowie!" they all
gushed as they showed me pictures of him. At the
time David was in his Ziggy Stardust phase, red hair
all spiked up. I asked, "What kind of thing is this?"
and they answered, "He's a new kind of thing, and
he's fabulous and we're all rich now!" Great.

Cherry Vanilla was a big part of this picture, and
I've got to say a word about her, because she's one
of my favorite people. Born Cathy Dougherty, she
was a pure work of art with a great laugh and big tits.
She was also really smart and the most openly sexual
woman I've ever met, with beautiful fire engine–red

hair and a wild nature. She'd perform her songs and
sing about her dream guy (it was Andy Paley at the
time; he's a famous record producer now, and was
everyone's dream guy at one time or another), and
the last line of the song was "and jerk off with the
handles of my brushes." [Applause.] Imagine a girl
singing about masturbating in a cabaret twenty-five
years ago.

Sex was a big joy for Cherry. You'd be at a party
and suddenly she'd be naked between two guys, in a
rimming sandwich! Her tongue would be up some
young guy's butt-hole, and when she pulled out to
breathe, she'd let out a whoop of happiness. Excuse
me, this was new. And as a Main Man employee, she
would give radio guys blowjobs in exchange for them
playing David Bowie's record. She'd walk into the
station and announce that she'd suck off anyone there
who could help her get this record on the air—and
she'd do it.

After all this advance hype, David Bowie came to
New York in 1972 for his debut American tour and
started meeting all the people he'd wanted to meet as
if it were an agenda to be gone through. Naturally
Leee introduced me to him, and David and his wife,
Angie, and I start hanging out together. They were
the nicest couple, though she was more like a business
partner and was in no position to object to David
picking up on another girl. By the way, David Bowie
is as heterosexual a male as I've ever known, though
he pretended to be much gayer than he ever was.
Whatever was happening at the moment was what he

felt he had to do, and gay was happening big time in the early seventies.

The second we met, we fell in love in a really sweet way. I was not quite twenty, and he was twenty-four. I hadn't slept with more than four or five guys when I met him. By then I knew how to get out before it got to that moment. To protect myself, I was more of a tomboy. And I wasn't interested in having sex, because I'd been used a few times back in Texas and not only did I not like the look on their faces, I didn't like the feeling I had. I only liked doing it with someone who loved me. For that reason the fags were the greatest thing that ever happened to me. No one tried to screw me, and I could dress up and party. And I was safer, so I thought. I didn't think of the psychological things that would come up from hanging out with fags, because obviously they have their own trip, and it's really not healthy for a heterosexual female to be tied into it. But for me, it was safety. *They* did all the drugs, sex, and booze, and I could live through them. All I had to do was look good and get my picture taken, and I got all the attention I didn't get as a child.

The closest time I ever saw to David Bowie acting homosexual was when we were on the road together. We were staying at the Beverly Hills Hotel. One night we went to the Rainbow Club and picked up this guy—I love picking up boys for other boys—who was really sweet and cute and brought him back to our bungalow. "Well, boys, I'm going to take a bath," I announced. I started the water running, but I peeked out through the bathroom door to see what was happening. I am a bit of a voyeur, I must admit. And they really didn't do anything—a little kissing, a little groping, touchy-feely, that's all. Not what I would call real sex by any means; certainly not what a real faggot would call real sex.

I have to admit that I pulled the "I'm going to take a bath" routine whenever David had girls with him, and those were the times I saw some real action. In fact, he once called me into the room to talk to him while he fucked a girl, because she was so stupid all he wanted to do was fuck her, and he needed someone to talk to, and that was me. I'd be watching the TV and talking with David, and he'd be screwing the groupie. Very nonchalant.

When it came to sex, Angie Bowie was much wilder than her husband. I've seen her crawling around on her hands and knees after having sex with a bodyguard, because it was so intense that she couldn't walk afterward. David would be in one room with me, and we'd be making love or we'd be talking while he'd be doing it with another girl, all on a kind of gentle level, and Angie would be in the other room making the floors shake.

Once I was with David and Angie came in, and we had kind of a threesome, the one big lesbian experience of my life. It was in David's bedroom at the Beverly Hills Hotel, and the two of us were lying in bed together, making out. I was wearing my standard T-shirt and panties, and he had long pants on and no shirt. Angie tapped on the door and opened it without waiting for an answer. "How sweet!" she cooed, no sarcasm, no jealousy. She really did think it was sweet.

It was very dark in the room, so I'm not a perfect eyewitness. Maybe "feel-witness" would be a better description. I know she went over to the foot of the bed and was rubbing my legs with one hand and, I presume, David's with the other.

"I've never done this before," I confessed to David.

First-time confessions only seem to get men more excited. He assured me that it would feel great, and that everyone should, after all, know what it's about. "Besides," he said, "you don't have to do anything you don't want to."

I think that was meant to be reassuring, though. I started wondering what kind of stuff I wouldn't want to do.

Then Angie began to move north. I was aware of some finger action down below, and I know it wasn't David, because his arms were around me, and we were kissing. The absolute decadence of kissing another woman's husband while she was there was so sinful that it was nearly intoxicating. Then his pants were off and Angie seemed pretty busy at the halfway point. I think she was giving David head and fingering him with one hand, while rubbing my most sensitive area with the other. It was all fingers, fingers, fingers. I never knew how much could be done with thirty fingers and three people, but it was an illuminating experience.

As I said, I couldn't see all the ins and outs of it,

but you can always gather what's being done by the nature of the moans and groans and giggles, not to mention what it feels like. Then Angie was up there, face-to-face with us, and we all kissed and licked one another. It was more interesting and curious than exciting. I guess it wasn't so hot for Angie either, because when she heard her giant-penised bodyguard come into the suite, she said, "Excuse me, lovies, that was just grand," and was gone. David and I continued making love as if there had been no interruption.

Just to create a ruckus, I told all the faggots I was having a thing with Angie. They were just dying. Not only was I screwing David, but Angie too (so I pretended). How could anyone be more "in" with the Bowies than that? When Angie came into Max's one night, I gave her a big, sexual kiss. I was so bratty. I thought I was really cool. If David could pretend to be a fag, I could pretend to be a dyke. Actually, I was getting a little out of hand. My attitude was going through the roof. I was no longer the shy, sweet girl I started out to be. I grew obnoxious. I blame it on the faggots. Live with queers long enough and you start picking up on their meanness. Now that's a terrible generalization, and I apologize to all fags who are not mean, but the ones who are know what I'm talking about.

Angie is a great woman, very intelligent and nurturing. She is the type of person who really cares about her friends, defending them like an angry mama bear. Apparently she had wanted David from afar

long before he knew who she was, and went after him
until she got him.

David once said, "I want to write you a song. What
do you want?" And I'm like, "Gosh, no one has ever
asked me that, I don't know, something like the Yardbirds, I guess," so he wrote "Jean Genie" with that
whole middle that's just like the Yardbirds. The guy
was amazing, creating this song right before my eyes
with his guitar and a little Pignose amp. The song is
not about me, but about Iggy, although I don't think
David was hanging around with Iggy yet. It doesn't
matter, it's a great song. I was in the "Jean Genie"
video, which makes me one of the first video bimbos.

I really cherish my time with David. When I knew
him he was a very tender guy, but I think he lived
his life on stage. When he invented characters, they
became an extension of something he wanted to be.
To me, he seemed more real as a performer than he
was in real life, though I found him to be a regular
guy, easy to get along with. I adored being with him.
He was never difficult or demanding, he was just
happy to be with me. We always had a good time,
and believe it or not, sex was secondary. Still, he was
a great lover, and we talked a lot during sex. He never
devoured me, though now it might be nice to be able
to say that he did.

I think I was food for his psyche, but he wasn't
one of those stars who needed to be flattered all the
time. I wouldn't have hung around with him if that's
what he had wanted. You can hire people to tell you
how wonderful you are, but he knew I was not for

hire from the start. Our first sexual experience was at
the Plaza. There had been a party in his suite. He and
Angie had separate bedrooms, and I remember that
there was lots of food still around. No drugs—we
never did drugs together. The bodyguards had been
dismissed, and we were alone, and I knew that we
were going to do it. Now, I wasn't there for just that.
I was there because I was part of the Warhol crowd,
and I happened to be a vivacious little nineteen-year-
old platinum blonde as well.

Yes, all our clothes came off, and yes, it was quite
passionate, though it was more comfortable than wild.
It was a natural progression from the way we already
felt about each other. And I never thought of taking
it further and becoming his mistress or, God forbid,
his wife. The next morning I borrowed a pair of his
pants to go home in, because I couldn't walk out of
the hotel in this strapless satin thing. It didn't take
long before the whole town knew about it. Not because I told anyone, but with an entourage the size
of David's at the Plaza, there's always someone who
knows exactly who is coming and going.

Leee found out about it that very day, and it was
a big triumph for him. "We got one in there!" he
crowed. After all, Bowie's manager was paying his
salary, and now he'd found David a little teenage
sweetheart. After that, I was at the Plaza all the time,
and so was everyone else, including Leee and Cherry.
Everyone loved it. I never had the feeling my friends
were using me to get to Bowie; I really think it genuinely made them happy to see us together. Now that

I'm older and wiser, I wonder. Well, however it happened, what did it matter? David and I clicked, and we wanted to spend more time together, and that's when he asked me to go on the road with him.

While he performed almost every night and rehearsed all day, I talked on the phone and waited for him to come back. The whole experience was like a giant, mobile tea party, with a stream of new playmates for Cyrinda. Everything was a tea party back then and with David and Angie Bowie, whoopie! Earlier I had mentioned Angie's bodyguard and lover, this black guy, Anthony Jones. He was a riot. He would come out of her room singing "Me and Mrs. Jones." He was fabulous-looking with skin like velvet, hazel green eyes, and a great English accent. One time Anthony and I were walking through the Beverly Hills Hotel down toward the pool where the little shops were, and I noticed all these women staring at him, and it was all because he'd pulled his giant cock out of his pants and it was just swinging along, halfway down his thighs. *You* try and look collected walking through the halls of a posh hotel with an exposed companion.

David and I had a cabana at that hotel, and we would sit there while Angie and the bodyguard fucked in the pool. *We* knew they were fucking, but to the chic women with daiquiris sitting around the pool, it looked as if they were doing some kind of swimming exercise together, this black man and this squealing blond woman. Paul Morrissey came over, picked up on it right away, and said, "I can't understand how you people get away with things like this." We were all rock-and-roll trash to him.

It was interesting to experience David and Angie's open marriage, but I never wanted that kind of relationship for myself. I'm usually very loyal because as I see it, when you sleep with other people, that's the end of the core relationship. You can be friends and sleep around, but not lovers.

Our affair lasted a couple of months and ended in San Francisco after the "Jean Genie" video. Tony DeFries hated me and wanted me out of the picture, especially if I wasn't going to do my hair exactly like David's, all red and spiky. He was furious that I wouldn't change my hair to match the Ziggy Stardust look. Can you imagine? He wanted everyone in the entourage to be a part of the Bowie thing.

My time with David had been a lot of fun, but the party was over. I was starting to feel like the boss's girl, and I didn't like it. On our last night together, I had on this long Lady Godiva wig which fell down to my knees and lots of pearls. I got into the bathtub and David was watching me. I said, "Oh, don't touch, I want to pretend I'm floating down a river." He had a robe on, and he dropped it and stood there and started to jerk off. I told him to try and come on the pearls, because I had read once that body moisture helps them retain their luster. It was so exciting. We were looking into each other's eyes when he came. It's cool watching a guy come. David Bowie shot all over me, all over the pearls, and into the bathwater. The next day I left. Did David ever have "the hots" for me? I doubt it. English people have a whole different way of looking at themselves and women, and I think I was a desirable commodity because I had all the right friends.

A short while after I returned to New York, I went to Roosevelt Hospital and found out I was pregnant with David's child. It was my first pregnancy and my first abortion. It was very nasty, and I was really sick for a few days. Nobody knew about it, not even Leee, because I wore a scarf and tried to go incognito. Abortions had only recently become legal at the time, and they asked you lots of questions: "Are you sure you want to do this? Why? Do your parents know?" Their questions were unbelievably intrusive, but I suppose, like most women, I was so glad that I could actually get an abortion that I wasn't terribly bothered by the bureaucratic inquisition. They asked me why I didn't want children, and I just told them it was an accident, a mistake. I was twenty years old, and I didn't think for one minute that I wanted to become a mother, even of David Bowie's child.

I still adore him. I saw him about two years ago in a restaurant, and we were so excited to see each other. But I have to tell you, his accent has changed a lot, and so has he. David is quite the gentleman now. "Hellow, hellow," he said, sounding so proper. His wife, the model Iman, must be turning him into a British aristocrat.

SIX

The Bridal Doll

In 1972, everyone who was anyone in the New York music and underground worlds went to see the New York Dolls whenever they played. Despite the fact that they were a complete commercial failure, they were a hot, tight band at the center of a major social and artistic world, playing regularly at the Mercer Arts Center, a suite of rooms in the old Broadway Central Hotel. The press loved them, especially Lisa Robinson, who was and continues to be an extremely powerful rock journalist/mover and shaker. Lisa regularly wrote about them in her columns in *Rock Scene* magazine, the hippest rock-and-roll publication of its time. It consisted mainly of picture stories with hilarious captions, and columns by such style-setters as Wayne County, who offered hilarious advice to teen-age boys about what kinds of stockings to wear with high heels. The same scene-makers were featured in every issue, so there came to be a *Rock Scene* cast of characters. Its circulation probably wasn't very high, and it didn't have the "prestige" of *Rolling Stone*, but

every musician and every musician wannabe in
America read it religiously.

So thanks to *Rock Scene* as well as the band itself,
the New York Dolls were creating a sensation. Besides being hot, they were outrageous looking. They
wore spandex, glitter, high heels, and makeup way
before it was acceptable for an all-male band to do
so. But when they appeared in virtually full drag on
their first album cover, they were labeled as a "bunch
of fags," and as a result committed commercial suicide. They were not fags, but it's hard to explain that
to your average American teenager.

The English are much more tolerant of drag, and
whereas David Bowie's career was launched by his
wearing dresses, the Dolls got their heads handed to
them on a platter. Although they were self-taught musicians and, by technical standards, terrible, they
sounded great! Other fledgling bands like the
Ramones would go and see them and say, "What are
we waiting for? To be better guitarists? Fuck it, look
at the Dolls! They can't play for shit but they've got
a record deal, and they're in *Rock Scene* every month!
Let's just start performing." And bands like the Ramones did and made history. Wherever they went,
people would say the same thing about them that they
said about the Dolls.

The lead singer of the Dolls was David Johansen,
who was tall, with long hair, a crooked smile, a deep
voice, and a heavy New York accent. Of all things
David possessed, one was his incredible stage presence. You probably know him today as his alter ego,

Buster Poindexter. He and the other Dolls used to
hang out at Max's, and I started going out with him.
I didn't love his band, but I didn't hate it either. It
was new music, and the lyrics were so great, each
song was so impressive, and each one of the Dolls
was fascinating in his own way. Most amazing was
the guitarist, Johnny Thunders. He never turned
around to face the audience while he played and he
had this big rooster hairdo and a plaid scarf. I really
loved the way he looked. It wasn't a fag's hairdo, it
was a straight guy's hairdo, but it was really spectac-
ular nevertheless. Still, it was David, the lead singer,
who captured my fancy.

What I liked about David was that he was young
and unpolished, and he was bringing rock and roll
into the family of Max's. It was a wild time. I don't
remember the moment David and I first met. It was
probably either at Max's or at the Mercer, and I
thought he was a snappy little talker, and Leee liked
him, and before I knew it we were tagged as the hot
new couple. *Rock Scene* got hold of us and our ro-
mance took on a life of its own in the pages of that
magazine. We were a famous couple before we even
thought of ourselves as a twosome.

I remember the first time David and I went out. It
was the summer of 1973. He brought me to his apartment on Third Street. He was living with some girl
at the time, and there were dirty pots all over, and
funky people as well, too funky even for me. It was
gross. There were bugs on the floor, and I couldn't
even bring myself to sit down. So we went to my

apartment on West 36th Street, and we screwed. I didn't intend to. I just wanted to get dressed up with him, but there we were, making love. I wasn't in love or anything, and I certainly wasn't jealous of whoever was living with him with her brown rice and cockroaches.

The next time we were together, I spent the night at his wretched apartment. I wanted to leave, but something made me stay. I think it had to do with that old Andy Warhol thing I mentioned earlier. I was rebelling against Andy's efforts to fix me up with men. Andy was furious about me and David being together. "Forget this guy," he said. "What are you doing to yourself?" And Paul Morrissey told me David was some kind of dwarf that was given hormone shots to make him grow. That only made me angry and made me want to hang out with David even more.

I don't know how long David and I would have lasted if people hadn't made such a deal about dumping him. He was a good man but not my cup of tea. I mean he was a pseudo-intellectual who read encyclopedias. Where's the scene in that? One of his best friends was Charles Ludlam, a little bald guy who'd put on a wig and play the title role in his own version of *Camille*, and that's just for starters. And I think it was Charles's influence that inspired David to bring that kind of theatricality to rock and roll.

Meanwhile, I was moving around all over the place. I lived with Ritty, the manager at Max's, off and on for a few months. Then I moved in with Allan

Stroh, who worked with the Allman Brothers and Jimi Hendrix. Allan had sublet Abbie Hoffman's apartment on Thirteenth Street, not far from Max's, a great apartment on the top floor. And Allan introduced me to this rich Iranian guy who gave me fur coats to wear on my dates with David.

David and I got along well, and Lisa Robinson kept the story going in her magazine, and we continued to be the king and queen of underground camp rock.

Those stories in *Rock Scene*! Photographs usually by Bob Gruen: CYRINDA GETS HER HAIR DONE, CYRINDA AND DAVID GO TO CHINATOWN, DAVID AND CYRINDA AT HOME (which was the campiest), CYRINDA AND DAVID GO SHOPPING FOR MUSICAL INSTRUMENTS AT MANNY'S. And we didn't know it then, but every guy in every band in America was reading every word of this, or rather studying every picture, because the captions were hysterical. David and I were setting the style for a large number of as-yet-unknown rock stars in America and England.

Paul Stanley later told me that Kiss used to read *Rock Scene* religiously, and I know that Aerosmith certainly followed everything the Dolls did. If you look at Aerosmith's first album cover, you'll see Steven Tyler in that little outfit, which was a complete rip-off of the David Johansen look. Meanwhile, the future Nancy Spungens of the world were basing themselves on me.

David had a bit of a drinking problem, but he was smart and easy for me to be with. He wasn't controlling, and he didn't try to order me around. We were the Couple of the Moment, and I liked the publicity and loved all the guys in the band. They were like a comedy act. And they were an alternative to the gay underground theater scene and the Andy Warhol uptown art and society scene, and it was fun, and it was definitely happening. Everyone in the group was drinking too much, and drugs also entered the picture. Heroin would certainly rear its head as far as this group was concerned, and it took its toll. In the meantime David and I were a couple, even though Leee tells me he remembers David taking out his cock and asking Wayne County if Wayne would like to feel it; but that wasn't a gay thing, it was David's shtick thing.

It was in 1973 that I first met up with Aerosmith. Their managers, Steve Leber and David Krebs, were the Dolls' managers. The two bands were rivals. The Dolls were incredibly hip and trendy and adored by the press, but commercially they were a failure. Aerosmith, on the other hand, was very unhip and loathed by the media, but by 1975, after the release of *Toys in the Attic*, they began to sell albums by the millions. I became friendly with Elissa Perry, the wife of Aerosmith's guitarist Joe Perry, and she convinced me that it was time I married David. "*Everyone* is getting married," she told me. "All the girls our age are getting married. You don't want people to think you're a groupie, do you?" That was a horrible thought. I definitely did not want people to think I was a groupie, so I decided to marry David.

Yes, I decided. David never proposed. I announced

one day, "I think we should get married now." And
he said, "Are you sure? I don't think that's really what
you want to do." He knew I was just doing it because
I thought it was the thing to do. David was dead set
against us getting married. Unlike me, he truly believed in marriage and knew it wasn't a game. I think
he went along with it anyway just to make me happy,
which of course it didn't.

I don't think there was ever much sexual attraction
between David and me, even in the beginning. At the
time I was still trying to define what percent of a
relationship was sexual, and I was having a difficult
time of it. I remember we were all at Max's and had
had too much to drink and this adorable boy walked
in. We made a bet as to who would get him first. I
wanted to win. I had to have a one-night stand with
this kid just to prove I could do it, even though I had
no interest in him at all. He had this little mod look,
with skin-tight satin pants, a short T-shirt, and a shag
haircut. Eventually everybody screwed him, and then
we dumped him on Angie Bowie. She figured if
everybody had been to bed with him, he must be
something special. And for her he *did* turn out to be
special. He moved in with her lock, stock, and barrel,
and she really dug him.

Nevertheless, David and I hung in there and three
years later were married at his family's church on
Staten Island. Leee walked me down the aisle and
kept saying, "It's not too late. You can leave." And I
wanted to leave, not because I didn't like David, but
because reality had hit home. "Christ, I'm in a fucking

church. This is actually happening." Suddenly I was
hit with a big-time case of the guilts, because it was
a Catholic ceremony, and there I was walking down
the aisle, lying with every step. I turned around and
looked out the back door of the church, and there was
a car sitting there, and I wanted to run so badly. If I
did, it would have been a fabulous drama. Imagine
that in *Rock Scene*! But for some reason, I went
through with it because I was too embarrassed to admit that I was making a mistake, which has always
been one of my big problems.

I was wearing a beautiful white-and-turquoise skirt
with a slit up the side and fabulous gray-and-gold
shoes that the famous illustrator David Croland had
made for me by the best silk people on Seventh Avenue. And I had a turquoise-blue tunic with big white
orchids. Afterward I changed into gray silk slacks and
a pink tunic. David got me a beautiful little platinum
ring, with little diamonds across the top, from Elissa's
mother's friend for only $100.

We went to his parents' house for a little reception,
then drove into the city and had a couple of drinks at
P. J. Clarke's. It was really boring, and I was over the
whole thing that very day. I knew it hadn't been the
right thing to do. I wanted to run away. I had made
the biggest, stupidest mistake ever, but it wasn't one
of the mistakes I could get out of right away.

Our day-to-day life got worse after we tied the
knot. I tried calling myself Cyrinda Johansen, but no
one would call me that except as a joke. Leee Childers would call and say, "Hello, is this Mrs. Johan-

sen?" Ugh. The marriage was such a travesty to everyone who knew me. I didn't even tell a lot of my uptown friends what I'd done. When they eventually heard about it, they couldn't believe it. Some of them stopped speaking to me because they thought I had done such a stupid thing. These were people who seriously believed that you marry a husband, you don't marry boyfriends.

My life as a newlywed was a nightmare. Some of my friends tried to be supportive. Lisa Robinson sent me beautiful pink towels with red initials, and David's family gave us several gifts, but I knew in my heart that my marriage was a joke. I was ashamed of myself, and our relationship went *whoosh*, right down the toilet. David started drinking more and I wanted out. David suggested we have children and I snapped, "Absolutely not! We can't afford it." His answer was that plenty of children sleep in drawers, and I said, "No child of mine will sleep in a drawer." (That was ironic, since a few years later I would be married to a millionaire, with a baby daughter, and there was no money coming from him to pay for milk, diapers, and heating our house! We'll get to that horror soon enough.)

Actually, David and I were scraping by well enough. I was doing some modeling, David was doing some gigs, he had a solo album in the works, and we knew how to get by. About this time I did Warhol's *Bad*. If you count John and Yoko's *Legs* as my first cinematic experience, and the "Gene Jenie" video as my second, then you have to admit that I hit the big time with number three, *Bad*. The movie is based on various news clippings of female crooks and murderers. It was directed by Jed Johnson. Pat Hackett wrote the script—she later edited the Andy Warhol diaries, and she is smart and fabulous. Carroll Baker was the female lead. She played a Mrs. Aitkens who ran a front that was an electrolysis parlor, but it was really a women's hit service. I am the first person seen on screen. I am walking across the street in Queens, with the Empire State Building behind me, and I am on my way to a diner, where I am supposed to order something to eat, then go into the bathroom and trash it.

I had to take a ketchup bottle and toss it around the bathroom, and stuff a toilet full of bathroom tissue to clog it, and then pull the magazine racks down. Naturally there were retakes, but they had to wash my dress every time because of the ketchup stains and wait for it to dry, so the shoot took a long time. The smell of the ketchup was nauseating. To this day, ketchup still makes me a little bit sick.

I know what they mean when they say most of making movies is just waiting. We had only one dress. It takes hours to do just the smallest thing.

Perry King was in the movie, and he was great. At one point we were in the trailer together, and it was very hot, and I was laying down with cucumbers on my eyes to refresh myself. They called me to the set, and Perry told me, "Never go the first time they call you. Never do that. Make them wait for you." I didn't have an affair with him, but I would have. I love him in everything. I did have a little crush on him. I can

understand why women have affairs with their leading men. It just works. It's just there. There's something about acting a part out. There's a scene in the
movie where Perry is lying on the sofa, and it's edited
to look as if I'm going down on him. It's a little
confusing to people because I was only supposed to
be looking at his ankle to see if he had a gun strapped
there. But people always ask me, "Were you supposed
to be going down on Perry King in that scene? *Did*
you go down on Perry King, ever?"

Well, no, to both questions. Oral sex is such a thing
unto itself, especially with men. I think it's just part
of the sexual experience. If you're with someone, and
you want to experience the whole person, you just
envelop them and certainly oral sex is part of that.
It's sensual, it's sensuous, and it certainly turns a guy
on if it's well-performed. I think sex is an art form.
The entire body becomes one sense. Feelings are so
heightened, and you see the other person just go completely out of himself, or completely into himself. It's
like another level of consciousness. You look in
someone's eyes, and you know they're just totally in
heaven on earth, and it's because of you. It's very
exciting, more so for men, I think, because men are
more physical. A woman needs something else, so
really for a man, if you're into making his entire
body, from the top of his head to the bottom of his
feet, feel sexually gratified, it's a great thing. I'm sure
most men would agree.

After wrapping *Bad*, though, I returned to my de-
teriorating relationship with David. The Dolls were

breaking up because two of them were heroin addicts who would later die from their drug abuse: Johnny Thunders overdosed on smack in New Orleans in 1991, and a year later Jerry Nolan died of spinal meningitis in New York, which I suspect was AIDS-related. Jerry had replaced Billy Murcia, the original drummer, who overdosed in 1972 on the band's first British tour. Still, considering a lot of heroin addicts worked for a living, and some very famous "old timers" were old-time junkies, I thought David should have tried to keep the band together.

So there we were, suffering along. I was miserable and David was going down the tubes with the Dolls. I can't really blame him, though. The Dolls just weren't happening anymore, and I was left with only him. There were no more diversions to keep us from actually getting to know each other, and I wasn't ready to face getting that serious, so I'd do things like paint the bathroom over and over. That's how stagnant our relationship was. So the bathroom ended up with two dozen layers of gray and silver paint, looking like something out of a Fritz Lang movie, and our marriage was in the gutter.

David's sisters would come around to visit the "newlyweds," and I don't think they liked it, either. Everyone knew that I was too flighty to settle down, raise a family, and go to Staten Island for Sunday dinners. And how right they were. One night I went out for a pack of cigarettes and never went back. I started seeing Steven Tyler, and his lawyers handled all the divorce stuff. My one-year marriage to David Johansen ended in 1977, on our wedding day.

SEVEN

The Courtship Begins

When I first saw Steven Tyler in the office of Steve Leber and David Krebs in 1973, his name meant next to nothing to me. I couldn't even understand who in the world would even want to talk to this person. He was so weird-looking. I had never seen anything like him. Here was this whacked-out, crazy-looking guy dressed like a court jester in the middle of Manhattan in broad daylight. He was wearing a velvet patchwork coat and had long, stringy hair, black stripes on his fingernails, and a teardrop on his face. I sat there with my mouth open, thinking, *What planet did this guy come from?*

I asked my friend Laura, who was working in the office, "What is *that*?" and she replied, "Oh, Cyrinda, that's Steve Tyler. He's going to be a big star, and we may be managing the band."

I laughed. *Right, this alien is going to be a big star.* But looking back now, I realize I was the one with an attitude, because Steven Tyler and Aerosmith had all the right elements. The group was like a heavy metal Canned Heat, and Steven's voice was very different—kind of boogie and country all rolled into one. Of course, it wasn't just the music. Steven Tyler has a presence and a charisma, and he has always been the type of singer whose voice and range could pull that special something out of a song and make it better.

Even though I hadn't heard of Steven Tyler, I had heard of Aerosmith.

They had been playing the club and college circuit up in Boston and had opened for the New York Dolls at Max's Kansas City in the early seventies. It was at Max's that Aerosmith, like other artists—Janis Joplin and Patti Smith, for example—auditioned for Clive Davis, the president of Columbia Records, who then signed them to their first recording contract.

The next time I saw Steven Tyler was at the Schaeffer Music Festival in Central Park. I was backstage taking care of photographer Bob Gruen's baby, Chris, when Aerosmith came offstage. Steven was then hanging out with Connie Grip, one of the most famous groupies, who was the girlfriend of the Dolls' bassist, Arthur Kane. So I'm sitting there staring at Joe Perry, and Steven stops in his tracks and stares at me. He looked so silly, like he didn't belong. He was far from sophisticated, and he did this music no one else was doing. Ironically, when we eventually got together a few years later, that's the thing I liked best about him and the band, because old-sounding rock and roll was what made me feel comfortable.

But to look at Aerosmith then, they looked like kids

fresh from the suburbs, with the exception of Steven, who looked like this crazy, mangy, funky clown. It was fruity. It was uncool, and I think that's what initially caught my eye, because God knows I didn't think he was good-looking. He was starting to get laid with some regularity around then, and naturally his idol was Mick Jagger. But Mick never looked like Steven; I think no other rock star in history did. Freddie Mercury came close, if anyone.

Steven has a body like a frog, I should add, for those of you unlucky enough never to have seen it all. He has a wide rib cage and shoulders and a small head. That's why he wore a lot of those scarves and puffed out his hair, because his head is so small. His hair is a lot thinner now than it used to be, and he recently tried hair extensions or weaves but didn't like them, I am told by mutual acquaintances, and had them removed. He's also been dying his hair, and I once told him that the dye job looked a little hard. "Oh, no," he said, "I don't want it to look too dyed. I don't want to look like Todd Rundgren."

Such a large torso, and the small hips go in, and then he's knock-kneed, so his thighs hit. He had a little butt, though cute. His body is pretty hairless, and he plucks out any hairs that appear on his chest or around his nipples with a pair of tweezers.

Now Joe Perry was a different story. He was truly sexy. I have photographs of him in his underwear, so it looks as if he is very well endowed. I think his dick may be bigger than Steven's (except for this one time when Steven's dick got so big that I had to take a

Polaroid of it. I think it was heroin that did it, but it only happened once. Usually heroin addicts can't even get it up). So Joe, Elissa, and I became friends while Joe and I had this silent love affair, which was very difficult.

Most of my contact with Aerosmith during the mid-seventies came through Bob Gruen, who was a very close friend of mine, and through David Johansen, John Lennon, and Lisa Robinson. Gruen was always doing shoots of Aerosmith because they were coming up in the world. One day in 1976 I accompanied Bob to the Record Plant where Aerosmith was putting the finishing touches on the album *Rocks*. That year, "Dream On," their first million-selling single, had been rereleased and had gone to number three on the charts. And *Toys in the Attic* was a monster. Believe me, I wasn't following the band's chart numbers then, but living in the music world, we all knew that this was a group rocketing upward.

At one point I was feeling a little dizzy because it was really hot at the Record Plant, so I left. I think Joe and Elissa Perry thought I was going off to do drugs, which to them would have been very cool. I really *did* need fresh air and was not doing drugs at all at the time, but still my dramatic exit impressed them. Very soon after that we started hanging out. I liked them—they were fun, they were new friends, and they got me to experiment with cocaine and heroin.

The punk movement was building steam in New York at that time, and I never liked the whole scene all that much. For starters, I hated the clothes. Dyed

black hair and studs were not for me. I wasn't wild
about the music, either; it all kind of left me cold.
And here were Joe and Elissa; they had money, they
were adorable. He always had leather pants on and a
cool shirt. She also wore cute clothes. In the summer
of 1976, I went to Boston and stayed with them for
a while. I was a minor rock-and-roll hotshot by then,
which is different from a groupie. I used to feel guilty
because I didn't fuck enough famous people, but I
found that I didn't have to sleep with these guys to
get into the scene. Rock and roll didn't equal sex for
me, it equaled music. If someone made music I liked,
that's what I was interested in.

Even though they were very sweet to me, I had
mixed feelings about Joe and Elissa. The drug thing
scared me, and they were into it heavily. Drugs were
still a sneaky, bad thing to do. When I later found
myself an addict, you can imagine what a low opinion
I had of myself, but back then, it was just dabbling.
No one in the Aerosmith circle could get close to Joe
and Elissa, but they latched on to me, and I was allowed into their secluded little universe. They'd become incredible prima donnas. I'd never seen
anything like their unmitigated ego-tripping. It was a
strange scene. Elissa was becoming my best friend,
I'm sexually hung up on Joe, and we're all doing
drugs. The other thing was I'd entered the Forbidden
City. The other people in the band and their girlfriends would stare at me and not say hello. It didn't
dawn on me until later that Elissa was keeping people
away from me.

I hung out with the Perrys whenever they came to New York; I'd take Elissa to stores that were hip. Of course, she had a lot more money than I did, because the band was really taking off then. On one trip Aerosmith was headlining at Madison Square Garden for the first time, and when I went to see the show, I ended up backstage, and that was the first time I actually spoke to Steven.

He was wearing a long, lacy outfit, and he was coughing up blood from the polyps in his throat that burst during the show. I really felt bad for him, so I talked to him for a bit, then moved on. A little while later I was walking by him, and he put his hand up so I couldn't pass. I was breathless, because for some reason, all of a sudden he looked really good to me. There was this masculinity, this high-school-boy-in-the-hallway demeanor about him that I stupidly picked up on, and he sensed it. I stood there talking to him, and I didn't know if he was going to try to lean in and kiss me, so I ducked under his arm and scooted away.

He just looked at me with a tough-guy look. By then he was getting lots of action, he was pulling groupies right and left. But I wasn't there to be pulled, and I suppose he saw that as a challenge. This was in 1976, and it was at this time that Elissa persuaded me to marry David Johansen. I think she wanted to get me out of the picture. I didn't know it at the time, but even though Elissa was married to Joe, she had this jealousy thing going with Steven that was extremely violent, nasty, and evil. When I saw it in action, I couldn't believe it. That night at Madison Square Garden, in the dressing room, Steven was about to sit down, and Elissa pulled the chair out from under him. I screamed, "Elissa, what are you doing?" I'd never seen anyone acting so rotten and with such attitude. They started fighting, and Steven grabbed the chair and smashed it into the wall. I was in shock. People didn't treat each other this way. They were supposed to be friends, because in the Dolls everyone was nice to one another. They had their little games, of course, but in the Dolls family we all loved one another.

I couldn't imagine a group of musicians and the people around them harboring as much hatred for one another as the Aerosmith entourage. And that was just the beginning.

Much later, I realized that what set Elissa off that night was seeing me and Steven talking. Steven's girls had never mattered because they were groupies, but when he and I started showing interest in each other, I became a threat to her dominance. If this sounds like the trashiest stuff on daytime TV, it was.

I still had the hots for Joe. He was strong and magnetic, and we really liked each other. We'd talk on the phone and I'd say, "If you ever want to come over, you should come," and he'd say, "Anytime you want me to come, I'll come." But we were both afraid of Elissa. And yet, who went berserk when I got together with Steven? Joe. It was wild. Elissa also got hysterical, because, I gather, she thought I was usurp-

Big sister, Lynda, and Cyrinda.

(Photo: Cyrinda Foxe-Tyler)

Tony Zanetta, Via Valentine, and Cyrinda appear in Warhol's play *Pork*.

(Photo: Leee Black Childers)

The New York Dolls (clockwise from top: Billy Murcia, Arthur "Killer" Kane, Johnny Thunder, David Johansen, Syl Silvain).

(Photo: Leee Black Childers)

Wayne (now Jayne) County, David Johansen, and Cyrinda.

(Photo: Leee Black Childers)

David, Jackie Curtis, and Cyrinda are looking randy.

(Photo: Danny Fields)

Cyrinda confers with The Who's Keith Moon.

(Photo: Bob Gruen)

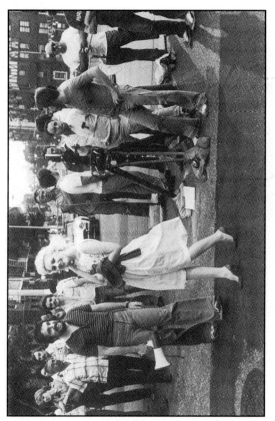

On the set of *Andy Warhol's Bad*.

(Photo: Bob Gruen)

Cyrinda and coauthor Danny Fields.

(Photo: Leee Black Childers)

Steven Tyler and Cyrinda at their wedding ceremony, September 1, 1978, atop Mt. Sunapee. Brad Whitford is at Cyrinda's right; Joey Kramer at far left.

(Photo: Cyrinda Foxe-Tyler)

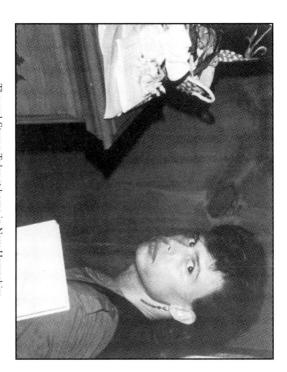

The real Steven Tyler at home in New Hampshire.

(Photo: Cyrinda Foxe-Tyler)

Joe Perry and Steven—"The Toxic Twins" in good times, 1973.

(Photo: Danny Fields)

Cyrinda and two-month-old Mia.

(Photo: Cyrinda Foxe-Tyler)

Axl Rose, Liv, Steven, and Mia backstage in 1987.

(Photo: Cyrinda Foxe-Tyler)

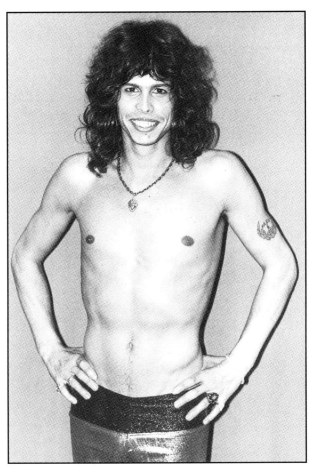

Steven Tyler.

(Photo: Danny Fields)

Room service, now! Hawaii, 1983.

(Photo: Cyrinda Foxe-Tyler)

Sing, baby, sing!

(Photo: Cyrinda Foxe-Tyler)

ing her position as the number one girl in the Aerosmith domain.

Amazingly, I don't think Elissa was jealous of me and Joe. She never knew about the underlying thing going on between us. Besides, I really felt it was improper to make a move on a married guy. I couldn't allow myself to do that, or even to admit that it was on my mind. Now that I'm older, I know that I felt very strongly about him and that he felt the same way about me. Does this sound crazy? Does this sound like a world too insane to make sense? Well, it was.

EIGHT

Home Tonight

After that violent scene backstage at Madison Square Garden, Steven dropped out of my life for several months, and Joe and Elissa Perry and I went back to being the Three Musketeers.

We were lonely without each other. Joe and Elissa would actually buy me plane tickets to join them on the road. They were very reclusive, very particular, and no one in the Aerosmith crowd was suitable company for them, so I was imported. When we were together, they didn't talk about anyone else in the band. It was as if the others were completely unworthy of conversation. The trips all over the country suited me well. I was bored and angry with my husband, David, and the Perry escape hatch was very attractive. And, of course, so was Joe.

I didn't see Steven again until 1977. David was doing some work in one of the studios, at the Record Plant, and Joe and Steven were fiddling with Aerosmith's *Draw the Line* downstairs in another studio. I went to visit Joe, and Steven seemed so inquisitive, so childlike, and I found him kind of appealing. Joe's attitude, on the other hand, was sort of proprietary: "This is *my* friend." So there was that little back-and-forth between the two boys. It didn't take much to bring out the rivalry between them, and let's face it, kids, I was hot stuff. Then my husband showed up and our innocent little bubble was burst. Reluctantly, I went home with David, but I think that the sparks between Steven and me became a little brighter that day.

A few months later came the great turning point, when everything started to click. Aerosmith was staying at the Navarro Hotel on Central Park South, and I was in Joe and Elissa's suite. Steven appeared briefly, and Joe told him to leave. I think Steven must have been very stoned and Joe knew it, but remember, any reason to evict Steven would have sufficed.

Steven protested. He was there to talk about music, and *I* was in the way. Joe retorted, "Too bad, just get the fuck out." So Steven left. A few minutes later, Steven comes back, this time with a legitimate musical question: Did anyone know the lyrics to "Milk Cow Blues"? Now that's an Eddie Cochran song that I knew very well from my brother's rock-and-roll collection, so I said that I did. And he replied, "Oh, that's just what I need, someone who knows those lyrics! Would you mind coming up to my room and reciting them so I can write them down?"

What could have been more innocent? So I said, "Sure I will," and Steven gave me his room number and left.

Joe had a fit. I had no idea how much these people hated each other. "You really shouldn't go, you know," he warned. "I really don't think you should go."

"Well, I'm just going to give him these lyrics, it's no big deal," I said, and besides, I didn't like being told where I could go and where I couldn't go.

"He's crazy," Joe continued. "Forget him, don't even talk to him, forget it, he'll get over it, he'll forget about it, he's so crazy he'll forget he even asked you. So don't worry about blowing him off, just stay here."

I couldn't help but think that this was kind of weird. Why were they so mean to him? They were so hard to each other, but of course I didn't know what forces were at play. So I said, "Oh, relax, I'll just go upstairs and talk to him for half an hour, give him the damn lyrics, and be right back."

I left and Joe was not smiling.

In Steven's suite all the windows were blacked out, the curtains were safety-pinned together, and all kinds of cloths and scarves and shirts were hanging over the lamp shades. It was dark and very strange; I learned later that sealing the windows is something that drug addicts do, which is part paranoia and part fear of daylight. This was the first time I was ever alone with Steven Tyler, and to protect myself on every level, I asked him to leave the door of the suite open. He couldn't believe that I would ask such a thing. "Well, I just think it's best," I said. "You being you, and me being me, people might think things were going on." The door stayed ajar.

I sat on one chair and he sat on a chair nearby. He had this puppy-dog look on his face and I was thinking, *Whoa! This guy is so cuckoo!* He took out a pad and asked me about those lyrics, and I started to recite them. Suddenly Steven said, "No, no, no! That's not right!"

And I said, "Yes, yes, yes, it is. I know it's right. I have the record at home if you'd like me to prove it to you." "No," Steven insisted, "that is not the way the Kinks do it." Some rock and roller this one is.

"Well, that could certainly be true, because I don't know how the Kinks do it," I said with kind of a sneer. "I thought you wanted the Eddie Cochran version, the *real* version." These guys had no idea of the roots of rock and roll. I would play old blues records for Joe and ask him if they sounded familiar, and he'd say, "Oh, it sounds like Jimi." Duh. I would say, "Where do you think Jimi got this stuff from? You know, Joe, you really should listen to the old stuff. They didn't make up rock and roll in England, you know; it started here."

The guys in Aerosmith thought everything started with Led Zeppelin, and I really had contempt for their taste and knowledge. "Milk Cow Blues" made it onto *Draw the Line*, by the way.

A few minutes later, Elissa was at the door. She must have been going crazy downstairs. She was carrying my purse and coat and looking like she was ready to kick the door down, but the door was open. Nothing was going on. Here she was, ready for a scene, had it all played out in her head, and there was nothing happening. It was like the sorcerer had been foiled. It was awful to look at her; she looked totally bewildered.

Backed by the satisfaction that I'd turned her thunder into a squeak, I came to her rescue. "I have to go now," I said to Steven. He didn't want me to leave, but Joe and Elissa were my friends, and I'd done what I said I would do, and just like Joe had predicted, he didn't know his ass from a hole in the ground, anyway.

I was being loyal to Elissa in her moment of misery, but I thought the whole scene was pretty disgusting. I wanted outta' there. She was getting crazy. I felt something very negative, and I didn't like it. When I got downstairs, Joe looked wiped out, as if Elissa had been torturing him about letting "their" friend go to the enemy. And I was thinking, *This is too much for me*.

Then Steven knocked on the door, yelling, "Let me in! Let me in! I have to talk to her!" Joe put the chain up on the door, opened it, and yelled through the crack, "No! Get out of here!"

Steven went away. A moment later he was back and pounding on the door again, but this time Joe opened it to find Steven with blood pouring from his mouth, yelling, "I'm bleeding, I'm bleeding. Let me in!" Joe turns around and goes to the kitchenette, gets a piece of rye bread, and throws it at Steven through the two-inch crack in the door. "Wipe yourself up!" he snarls.

I shifted into my most civilized mode. "Please, Joe,

you'd better let me talk to him. This is getting ridiculous." *Getting?* Steven's out in the hall going berserk. He picks up one of those hallway ashtrays with the sand in them and throws it at the door. *Crash!!* At that instant I stopped liking Steven. I stopped liking Joe. I stopped liking Elissa. I wanted to go home! Finally, when I was on the verge of hysteria, Joe took off the chain and let Steven in. Elissa was stomping around, throwing things on the floor, while Steven and Joe were talking about meaningless bullshit. It was time for me to go. I couldn't get out of there fast enough.

Of course, looking back now I see the insanity was all drug-induced. Or let's say the drugs enhanced what was really going on. But it was all too intense. I seriously thought about never seeing any of these people again, but that didn't last too long. Joe and Elissa were the center of my life, and soon there was another plane ticket for me to join them. It was the fall of 1977, around the same time I left David. I went to Kansas to join Aerosmith and never looked back.

At that time Aerosmith was still enjoying the great success of their 1976 album, *Rocks*. When the Perrys invited me, they asked that I bring some leather pants Joe had made for himself at Skin Clothes in New York. Years later—this would be funny if it weren't so outrageous—Steven claimed, during our divorce proceedings, that I was bringing drugs to Joe Perry under the guise of carrying pants. According to my husband, I was the heroin courier. The truth is, I don't know if I did or not. I certainly wouldn't have done it knowingly. The thought of getting arrested was too scary. I couldn't have coped with it.

In Kansas I stayed in a hotel suite with the Perrys, with my own entry out to the hall. We were on a different floor from Steven, which is apparently how they liked it. One night I heard this scratching on the door. It sounded like a little dog, but when I opened the door it was Steven. He was sitting on the floor, scratching the door and playing with the little rubber pad that keeps the door from making a hole in the wall when you open it. *Boing, boing, scratch, scratch.* There he was, sitting in a heap, with this helpless look on his face.

"What are you doing?" I asked. He said he wanted to come in, and suddenly Joe was in the hall, yelling, "No! You can't come in! She's married, and I'm protecting her. Get away! You can't have her. I told David I would watch out for her." The situation was beyond absurd. Joe was protecting me from Steven, but not because he had made any promises to David. He was protecting me because he was wild about me and being driven insane by his loony wife.

The next episode with Steven was far more intense. This was in Las Vegas several weeks later, in November. I had my own room, courtesy of Joe Perry, and one night Steven came by with two Seconals. I took them and passed out. I really don't know why I took them, except he said something like, "Here, these will make you feel good." Well, they put me out. And when I woke up, he was lying on the bed next to me. He said he hadn't touched me. He said he just wanted to lie down near someone for a while and then go to dinner. He seemed different, even exciting. I was going through a big change; I guess I was falling in love.

All of a sudden he was not as goofy-looking as before. He seemed more interesting. I was looking at him more closely and he said things to me like, "You and I would have beautiful children. I want you to have my children." I made a joke out of it and inspected his teeth like I would a horse for breeding purposes. "Nice teeth," I told him. "It's a possibility." He didn't know what I was doing, of course, and I had to explain it to him, and the joke was lost. That's the thing about Steven. He never gets the joke. But that night with the Seconals, he was very courtly and extremely charming. What also improved matters considerably was the fact that Joe and Elissa were not around to make a scene. It was nice to see him out of the context of the big battles with the other two.

By then, being on the road with Aerosmith had become my life. The style in which the group traveled was not unappealing to me. That same year at the Beverly Hills Hotel, Joe and Elissa had one of the dozen luxurious bungalows, in which I had my own bedroom, bath, and a separate entrance. One night Steven came to visit me, and he was acting bossy and a little rude, and I got uppity and said, "You have to leave. Go now, get out!" I had said something about my underwear disappearing (things always disappear on the road; it happened to all my jewelry eventually) and Steven made some lewd remark about Joe probably taking my underpants and jerking off with them over his face. I didn't think anyone should talk to me that way, and so I chased him out.

Steven wasn't staying at the Beverly Hills Hotel. It was too sedate and plush for his taste. He preferred the more modern and sterile L'Ermitage. After being ejected from my room, he found himself on the grounds of the hotel without a car and driver at his disposal. I have a feeling he figured it was easier to return, apologize, and try to get laid than to find a cab back to his own hotel. So he came back and scratched at my door like he had done at the hotel in Kansas. We made up, and it was kind of sweet. My surrogate "parents," Joe and Elissa, were at the other end of the bungalow, and I was feeling frisky. When I let him in, I was not dressed seductively, but as a perfect little Catholic girl in my cotton underpanties and T-shirt. We were talking small talk, and it started getting a little romantic when he said, "I kinda like you," and I said, "I kinda like *you*, too." He suggested we lie down and cuddle, and we did. I felt really safe with him. We were talking when he finally said, "Enough of this!" and jumped on me.

The evening was very tender. There had been so much leading up to it. He was considerate and giving, unlike the "Do everything to me while I stand (or lie) here like I'm the master and you're the slave" mode he got into later in our relationship. He was wearing just a bathing suit and a T-shirt, and we undressed each other and looked at each other's bodies without saying anything for a few minutes. Then I reached over and turned off the light, and we made love. It was not every-which-way position, and not even any oral sex that first time, just classic late-adolescent male-female sexual intercourse. And we worked quietly, because Joe and Elissa were under the same roof, which made it more fun. It wasn't just a fuck, it was sweet, like doing it the first time in high school.

We were so immature—at least I certainly was. And he was used to all these groupies, these girls with their clothes ripped off, lying spread-eagle and waiting for him to penetrate. I was this woman on her own trip, and he'd been chasing me around the country, and I'd been hanging out with his best friend and biggest rival, and he'd been going nuts. I had seemed unattainable, I suppose.

That night I fell in love with Steven Tyler. We came together and fell asleep in each other's arms. When we woke up late the next morning, Steven insisted that we go into the living room together and confront Joe and Elissa as lovers. He was crowing with pride: "I saw you with David, and I got you! I wanted you and I got you!" Well, it was nice to feel *that* wanted.

We went in holding hands. For the occasion, Steven had done his hair up in this weird 1950s hairdo. Joe and Elissa looked at him like, "What is this?" and they just freaked. She went ballistic and instantly became the worst enemy I had ever had. She called the group's manager, David Krebs, and insisted that he personally break us up. David arranged to have dinner with Steven and me, and at dinner he said, "You know, Elissa called me and is complaining about you two, but forget it, I don't want to talk about it." He was used to Elissa's complaints and demands and had been ignoring them for some time. He certainly didn't see me as she had described—as a menace to the band.

I was Steven's princess. He made me call my mother. It was hideously awkward. I babbled something about having met Mr. Right. Then he called his mother and said, "I've finally met the woman of my dreams, and she's just like you." I'd never met his mother, or I'd have ended our involvement immediately upon hearing him make this invidious comparison. Then he made me call David, who said, "Oh, yeah, okay." I know he had to have been hurt, but at the same time I think he was glad that I was out of his hair.

We started going together in December of 1977. It was a done deal. Steven was taking me home with him to his house in Brookline, a prosperous suburb of Boston. My stuff was still at David's apartment in New York, but Steven told me not to worry, and I didn't. "You'll have all new things soon enough," he promised. My friends in New York told me, "Oh, Brookline is very nice, it's a good neighborhood."

I had been to Joe and Elissa's house a year earlier, and it was perfect. It was on Wobin Hill in Newton, another nice suburb, a 1920s Tudor-style home, big living room, dining room, balcony, not grandiose, not pretentious, but a nice little gem. And this was only

the lead guitarist—imagine how the singer must live!
I was very excited.

Aerosmith flew back to Boston from Los Angeles,
then separated at the airport. Steven's Jeep was waiting for him there, and the two of us drove off to my
new home in rock-and-roll big time. It was late, very
cold, very dark, with snow on the ground, and we
pulled into the driveway of a huge white house, stunning, all lit up, and I was thinking, *Oh, divine! After
all those tiny apartments in New York, a mansion at
last! Space at last!* Well, we kept driving past the
house, then behind it, and there was Steven Tyler's
home, behind the woodpile, a converted carriage
house, a garage. My heart sank, but I was in love,
and everything would be okay.

Something not okay happened right there and then.
Steven got mad that no path had been shoveled to the
door of his home, and he became furious. He was
stomping and cursing, and he took his huge boom box
from the back of the Jeep and smashed it on the ice.
Oh well, my new boyfriend has a bit of a temper, this
wasn't news, but it scared me. There we were, starting
a new life, and the guy has a violent tantrum the first
night at our new home.

Yes, the new home. You walked directly into the
kitchen, full of dirty plates and an old juicer covered
with crusty spinach. He'd always had people living
there, doing things for him, and I guess he'd called
ahead and told them to clear out because he was coming home with his New York princess. It looked as if
the house had been abandoned in a hurry. It was re-

ally funky, filthy, and disgusting. Now it was my turn
to have a fit, because as soon as I said something
about the dirtiness of the place, Steven responded
with, "So you'll clean it up."

I can't describe it. It was like no place I had ever
lived in or seen in my life, and I had been in a few
truly grubby coldwater flats on the Lower East Side.
This was the grubbiest place I knew, and the person
living there from now on was me. Here was a guy
who was presumably a millionaire, and he was living
on a very low level of style and taste, indeed.

But let me finish describing the rock star's digs.
The kitchen door was the only usable entrance. There
was a front door, but it was sealed shut. The furniture
consisted of a large brown velour sectional and a big
dresser with cardboard backing. I saw a clock radio,
a TV, a very ugly carpet, a fireplace that sticks out
into the middle of the room, and no chairs. The only
bathroom was upstairs, near the bedroom. In the bedroom, the beds had been dismantled and the mat-
tresses leaned against the wall; the room was used for
storage. There were some towels hanging in the bathroom that neither looked nor smelled very fresh.
Steven built a fire. We slept on the velour sectional,
on some sheets I found upstairs.

I was heartbroken. He was living like a poor person. He never elevated his way of living when he
made money; he just acquired more crap, or what
looked like crap. He could buy a $3000 sofa and
make it look like it cost $299. This was not the home
of a rock star, much less a rock star's wife-to-be.

When we woke up the next day, he went in to "inspect" the kitchen and yelled at me because it was still disgusting. How was I going to cook in it if it hadn't even been cleaned? Cook? Clean? I was thinking, *What have I gotten myself into?* and he's yelling, "Who do you think you are, you fucking bitch?"

I shot back, "Wait a minute. Who do you think *you* are? I know who I am. Do you know who I am? Do you remember? I'm someone you wanted to be with, someone you fought for and were so proud to show off in front of your big rival, Joe Perry. What was all this for? What is happening here?"

I was crying, I was so miserable. He said, "Why don't you get back on a plane and go home to New York?" and he wrote me a check for $1200.

I said, "Fuck you! Shove it up your ass! I'll walk back to New York before I take your fucking money!" and I threw the check back at him.

We were off and running. I didn't go back to New York. I had no place to go. I was too embarrassed. Besides, there were four factors that mitigated the situation. One, he became contrite pretty fast after I threw the crumpled check back at him: "Okay, okay, listen, I have an idea, we'll go shopping," he muttered. That prospect always cheered me up. To this day, when he talks about the good times we had together, they always involve shopping and expensive presents. Two, this carriage house was temporary. The lease was running out, and he told me we were going to move to his "estate" in New Hampshire, a large lakefront property he'd bought where he was building his dream house. Three, we were going to be on the road with the band most of the time anyhow, and "nesting" did not loom large in the coming year's schedule. Four, and most important, I was so much in love with him and so full of hope that everything was going to be wonderful.

The two months we spent in the carriage house were a nightmare. I had no idea of the extent of Steven's drug dependency until the dealers started coming around. Soon the house was crawling day and night with the creepiest, ugliest drug dealers and trashiest whores. I had only dabbled in cocaine and wasn't into it yet, and so I'd be tired whenever he'd be wired, and there was no place to hide. Whenever I opened a closet or a cabinet, I'd find a stash of cocaine in some novel container—a peanut butter jar, a baby food container, a coffee cup—plus there were Seconals and Tuinals. I would dump everything I found down the toilet, but not fast enough to stop the flow of drugs into the house.

Steven would pass out on the floor, totally fucked up from all the cocaine and the pills, and the dealers would go through his pockets for money while I screamed, "Get out of here!" He'd wake up and accuse me of being involved in some suspicious activity, and I'd be washing his underwear by hand in the sink, because there was no washing machine. What could I do? This was really early in our relationship. There was no child, I wasn't pregnant yet, and I could have walked. But I couldn't admit to myself that I'd made this terrible choice. I was so ashamed of myself, so embarrassed.

NINE
Sight for Sore Eyes

From the start I should have seen, and understood, that Steven was too rugged for me. The girls he'd been with were also rugged, and inexpensive, easy-to-keep people. I was and still am a high-maintenance, high-strung female. His other girls were probably used to being subservient. Me? I'd never even learned how to make macaroni and cheese. In my entire life I'd never cooked. I had not been brought up to wait on a man in any way. Now I was a maid in a hovel in Brookline, Massachusetts.

I spent hours each day bawling my eyes out. I had a lot of grief just about being stuck in Boston, or rather a suburb of Boston. What the hell is Brookline? You can't just go out and walk around, you can't just hop on a train. This was not the same as being in a city, intelligently mapped out and easy to get around. In Brookline you had to have a car or you had to call for a taxi, you couldn't just hail one. I didn't know how to get to Tom and Terry Hamilton's house in

Newton. So I'd do nothing but clean his fucking house all day long.

Steven owned a little converted Cessna six-seater that he kept in New Hampshire, flown by a former World War II pilot and his son. He had always wanted to rent it out to hunters, but he never did, so it just sat there. When I persuaded him that I needed to go to New York to get my dog, which was still at David Johansen's apartment, he had a limo pick me up in Brookline and take me to the Boston airport, where the plane was waiting to fly me to New York. Then another limo was waiting in New York, which brought me to David's, where I let myself in (I had called David ahead of time to tell him I was coming), got the dog, got back in the limo, boarded another plane, got into another limo, and went back to the squalid hut behind the woodpile. What's wrong with this picture?

Finally we moved to New Hampshire. Actually, we were evicted from the Brookline house for not paying the rent (and I'm sure for other things that were not specified to me) before the lease was up. It was February 1978, and we were headed toward the dream house about which I'd heard so much. We flew up there, and the Jeep was waiting at the local airstrip. Steven and I drove together to our new paradise.

The property was seven hundred feet of lakefront, and a couple of hundred feet up a hill. A little dirt road went through the property. The house was being built on a platform that extended out over the water (too far out, it was later discovered, when the lake started seeping inside for occasional visits) and was far from ready. Our residence was to be a little gray house, creatively called the Gray House, where grain was stored. As we drove toward this Shangri-La in the freezing darkness, Steven said to me, "Do you know where we are?"

I said, "How on earth could I know where we are?" And he said with a grin, "You're on the lake!"

He'd been driving on the goddamn frozen lake in front of the goddamn unfinished house. We could have gone through the ice and perished at any minute, and he was laughing hysterically. It was pitch black and we started to skid, and he began laughing even more maniacally. He kept trying to make the car do a 360-degree spin. The fear and weirdness of it all was too much, and I started to cry.

The Gray House was a little boxy hut, with bright orange shag carpeting and burgundy walls, that gave new meaning to the word *cheesy*. It wasn't a log cabin kind of thing that you'd see in the movies, but a white-trash bungalow. Upstairs was a bedroom for storage and two other little bedrooms. Everything was in burgundy and orange. There were trees surrounding the house, so closely that there was hardly any light during the day. Steven thought the big house was going to be finished within the next six months, by the end of the year at the latest, but it wasn't. Actually, it was so badly planned and executed that it may never be finished. It was a huge cocaine playboy mistake from the very beginning.

In any case, it would be a long time before we

moved in, so I tried to convince myself that the whole scene was utterly charming, right out of Currier and Ives. Nobody was working for us there—it was winter, dreary and dead—but with a lot of touring coming up, and the completion of the Big House seemingly so imminent, I wasn't all that annoyed.

At the first opportunity, I was shown the inside of the Big House, or what there was of it, and it was so totally empty that I thought, *What a great place for sculpture!* I had visions of Louise Nevelson masterpieces strategically placed in this huge space, but that was never to be. Just meeting the workmen was a downer. I did not get along with the architects and the electricians and all the rest. They were not New York–quality workmen; I could pick up on that just by talking to them. I hadn't had much experience with builders, to be sure, but there was something shoddy about their whole approach. Maybe their boss was the real shoddy entity in that project.

At one point I was unpacking and came across a picture of me and David Johansen, which drove Steven bananas. Right there and then, he insisted that I call David and tell him I was never coming back. "I think he knows that by now, Steven," I assured him, but he wasn't satisfied. Also, he happened to be holding a shotgun, so I was not inclined to argue.

While I was on the phone with David, Steven began firing the shotgun out of the window of the Gray House, shooting into the trees. "What is that noise?" David asked, and I said, "Oh, it's nothing, just Steven shooting his shotgun out the window. Why would you ask?"

I don't know why Steven made me phone David, or why he was shooting the gun; I still don't get it. When David heard I was planning to stay forever with this nut who was shooting a gun out the window, he knew I was in deep trouble. He started telling me about some potent new Vitamin B complex. I thought it was some sort of joke, but it's the vitamin they give to drug addicts, and in fact it's one of the things that helped me a lot when I fought my own heroin problem a couple of years down the road.

I was trying to figure out how to cope with this really funky guy while living in a granary and building a cardboard mansion in the middle of nowhere. He has to have the most expensive house in the least expensive neighborhood. He never moved up, never bettered himself. My daughter, Mia, showed me a picture of the house he lives in now, in someplace called Marshville, Massachusetts, and nothing has changed.

There was a lot of touring planned for the band for early 1978, so Steven and I escaped from New Hampshire and headed for the West Coast before the winter got too oppressive. Our first stop was to meet his parents, who were visiting with his sister and her then-husband at their house in Philadelphia. It was a short visit, not memorable, and certainly not especially pleasant. I didn't like the looks of these people, having cocktails in the middle of the afternoon, smoking cigarettes—what my mother would have called "loose."

I was nervous about being with Steven and his mother. I had heard him on the phone with her, and he would say things that I could never imagine anyone saying to a parent. I don't know what her part of the conversation was, but on his end it was "fucking this and fucking that," and I was so embarrassed I left the room. He'd be cursing and screaming at this poor woman, and it gave me the shakes. On the phone he could be really mean. Of course, he could be the same in person, but on the phone there were no boundaries, no reservations whatsoever. He'll say anything. He has no sense about how one human being should treat another. I never saw him talk this way to his mother face-to-face; in person, they always cuddled and smooched, which was almost worse. Never in the course of our relationship did we spend more than a few consecutive hours with his family. On this introductory occasion, we were out of there in ninety minutes and back in our hotel. He never asked me what I thought of his family, and I never told him. Nor did he ever tell me what they thought about me. It's just as well.

The year 1978 began with Aerosmith's most recent album, *Draw the Line*, peaking on the charts at number eleven. *Toys in the Attic*, released in 1975, also peaked at eleven, but it was their breakthrough, stayed on the charts forever, and was followed in 1976 by the very successful *Rocks*, which got to number three. It's the curve as well as the bare numbers, they always say in the music business, and Aerosmith's curve had seen its peak and was heading downward. Critics and the public in general gave a thumbs down to *Draw the Line*, which I happen to think is an underrated album. Nevertheless, the trend didn't turn up again until the late 1980s, when the group made its miraculous "comeback," no doubt the biggest in rock history, but I'd been moved to the sidelines by then. In fact, in a strange twist of irony, the album that sealed their comeback triumph, *Permanent Vacation*, reached number eleven the month Steven and I were divorced.

Draw the Line is also considered the beginning of the band's decline, because drugs were turning their stage shows, for the most part, into a poor excuse for rock and roll. And the band, in conjunction with their management, had participated in the uncontrolled growth of their touring expenses. It had all become a bloated, inefficient organization that was doomed to lose money. At each stop, for example, their private jet was met by five limousines, one for each member of the band. When I first saw that, I was stunned. It was like the president was in town. But it was only because they hated each other so much and no one said no.

The group had two major gigs on the West Coast: an appearance in Robert Stigwood's movie version of *Sgt. Pepper's Lonely Hearts Club Band*, followed by the California Jam 2 Festival. Steven and I went to Hawaii first to thaw out. It was very luxurious. We flew first class from Boston to Honolulu via San Francisco, then were met by a real estate agent, who gave us the keys to the house we'd be staying at on Maui.

A chartered plane took us there, and we had drivers and servants. This was more like it. It was a great big white house, surrounded by red clay, all raked and elegant, and of course Steven scored a large quantity of Maui Wowie, the infamously potent local pot.

I never liked pot. It induces paranoia in me, and this time I started having Sharon Tate hallucinations. I was terrified that madmen were going to come in through the windows and kill us, then I was afraid I would forget to breathe and just die. My being needy bored Steven. After all, he was the only one ever allowed to be needy. But he didn't hit the roof. He just got mildly annoyed and said, "Just go to sleep. Everything is going to be all right." That did make me feel better, and there was a closeness between the two of us that was as good as it ever got. We were still falling in love.

Steven's part in the *Sgt. Pepper* film involved him being thrown off a cliff by the Peter Frampton character and dying. But he refused to die in the movie at the hands of Peter Frampton because he thought it would be bad for his image, so they rewrote it and Steven got killed by the Strawberry Fields character. He insisted on doing his own stunt, which didn't make the producers happy. This was a professional set, and here was a guy with a wild reputation wanting to take a thirty-foot leap. So they were really nervous.

I was supportive of his decision. "I want to do it," he told them. "I can tumble, I can do it." I'd never seen him so happy about anything as he was about doing that leap onto an air cushion. He was exhilarated, and I loved watching him doing it, and I was happy that he was happy. I thought maybe he'd be in a good mood that night. I also loved being there because all the fag hairdressers and makeup artists worked on me just for fun, and it reminded me of the old days in New York, being attended to by those fabulous queens.

For me, the strangest part about being on the *Sgt. Pepper* set was seeing the Bee Gees. They were like characters from a cartoon. But Peter Frampton was divine, one of the sweetest people I've ever met in the music business. It was a big open studio, no trailers, rows and rows of makeup mirrors, casual but tightly run. The movie, as everyone knows, was a complete dog, with the exception of Aerosmith and their performance of "Come Together," which I think is better than the Beatles' version. It was a big hit for them later in the year.

Next on our California agenda was Cal Jam 2. It was on March 18, 1978, and it was as horrid in its way as *Sgt. Pepper* was nice. I had been so excited about the scope of the show. I thought it was going to be a mini-Woodstock. They had the whole band staying at the same hotel for this event, because they all had to be scooped up and brought to the site precisely on time. Everything had to be perfection. The crowd was going to be in excess of a quarter of a million people.

My anticipation had turned into dread as a result of Steven's behavior in the days immediately preceding the concert. We were staying at L'Ermitage, not my favorite hotel, and we were fighting a lot. The screaming was so loud that even Richard Harris, our next-door neighbor and a notorious drunk who frequently gets thrown out of hotels himself, complained to the management. Aerosmith's managers thought it was all a big joke. Steven was really on edge the week before Cal Jam, and anything could set him off.

I was turning into a nervous wreck, too. One afternoon I was trying to get into my room, and the combination-key thing wasn't working, and suddenly I see Waylon Jennings coming down the hall in my direction, absolutely stoned, bouncing from wall to wall, and he saw me and started to charge at me like a bull. I was scared to death—it was like being in the path of a freight train. Just as Waylon got within a yard of me, the door across the hall opened and Henry Smith, our road manager, pulled me inside to safety. I broke down in hysterics. An overreaction, I admit. I mean, what harm could darling old Waylon Jennings do? I think it was really my fear of Steven that induced the hysterics, because he was always having temper tantrums, always freaking out, always pounding the shit out of me. The door I was having trouble getting into? Steven later tore it off its hinges during one of his outbursts. We were not loved by the management of L'Ermitage, let me tell you.

The night before Cal Jam, Steven and I went to the house of some music business manager in the Hollywood Hills, and the two of them left me alone in the house with some spaced-out bimbo while they went into the pool shed. I was watching through the window of this dark, gloomy, unkempt house, and I see Steven emerge from the pool house, naked except for a towel around his waist, and start hippity-hoppitying around. I don't know how else to describe it. Hippity-hoppitying, like those elves with horns and goaty legs in Aubrey Beardsley's drawings. I'd never seen him do that before.

I called out to him. "Steven, we really have to go. It's after two o'clock, and we've got a big show tomorrow."

"Shut the fuck up! Shut your fucking mouth!" he shouted back. "Who the fuck do you think you are?"

I was really scared. Steven was as far gone as I'd ever seen him. Whatever drugs they were doing in that pool house, he must have inhaled a massive dose. We got back to the hotel just as it was getting light.

The next day we separated into boys and girls for the helicopter ride to the Ontario Speedway, where the concert was to be held. When we got there we were taken to our trailers. Steven was a basket case. I was so sad. He was so zombied. He was upset that we'd been separated into two helicopters, but I was so glad to have a break from this monster. This day would be one of the most infamous of his career. I have never read a book about Aerosmith that did not contain the story of the reporter who tried to interview Steven at Cal Jam and found him in his dressing room, snorting huge piles of coke that were lined up on a photo of him from a Japanese fan magazine.

That's one of the images for which he will always be remembered.

Steven was too out of it to do his stage makeup. When I went near him, he punched me in the head. I ran out of the trailer. The band's set was bad. Steven was so weak he could hardly breathe, and I was overcome with anger at him for being so unprofessional in front of this gigantic crowd. I was on the side of the stage, watching the show and dying inside. He had insisted that I be put somewhere where he could see me, and if he didn't he'd stop the show and ask the roadies where the fuck I was. That pathetic fucking little addict—you don't fuck yourself up before appearing in front of the largest crowd you've ever played to. It was utterly inexcusable.

After Aerosmith's performance, everything went downhill. The cocaine was really hitting, and now Steven was going from zombie to maniac. In the catering trailer, he picked up every bowl of egg salad, tuna salad, whatever, these big heavy glass punch bowls, and smashed them against the walls. I was hiding under one of the tables behind a paper tablecloth, and Joe Baptista, who worked for us, God rest his soul, came and got me out of there. I would have been hurt severely if I had stayed around. Steven trashed that trailer so badly that Bill Graham, who was promoting the show, sent him a huge bill for it. Bill Graham got nothing but respect from the musicians he worked with; if he didn't respect you, you had to be at the low end of the loathsome scale.

Before the show, everyone was trying just to get

Steven dressed and onto the stage. Afterward, he had
to be subdued. What a dirtbag. Eventually some big
bodyguard would come and wrap him in something
and take him away. He'd get very passive then and
turn into a rag doll. He'd beat the shit out of any
woman, but if a big guy came in and said, "Okay,
enough, Steven," he'd yield and just go along with
him.

Before heading south after Cal Jam, we went back
to New York for a meeting with Steven's managers,
Leber and Krebs. It was March 26, 1978, Steven's
thirtieth birthday. Guess what his managers gave him?
A box of cupcakes. I am not kidding. Their biggest
star, their biggest moneymaker (after all, they took
their percentage of Aerosmith's gross revenues, and
Aerosmith's recording deal with Columbia Records
was actually a Leber/Krebs deal in which Aerosmith
was in the role of subcontractor), and they give him
a box of cupcakes. He was genuinely sad, and I felt
bad for him. They weren't even gift-wrapped, and
when they were handed to him, he looked at me with
that puppy-dog stare that had been my undoing in the
past. I could tell Leber and Krebs were not pleased
with Steven Tyler. Aerosmith was turning out to be
something less than a party ride, and he was certainly
not as much fun as they thought he was going to be.
Still, not being adored made Steven morose. Not
having a big party with hats and horns hurt Steven.
At thirty, he was still such a child.

I tried to make it up to him. I took him shopping
at Skin Clothes on Lexington Avenue and bought him

lots of marvelous leather stuff, then to Bergdorf's before returning to our suite at the Plaza, where we ordered room service and champagne. We were giggly and lovey, and he suggested that we try something different that night. I thought it would be cute to tie him to a bedpost, like St. Sebastian, naked except for the Bergdorf ribbons, and go up and down his body with my tongue. I did him that night like I'd never done him before. Thirty should be a special birthday, you know.

After he came, he said, "Well, untie me now." And I said, "No, not yet," and while he was tied up, I told him how much I loved him, and how I'd always be there for him, no matter what. He didn't mind letting me have control of this particular situation, and he said he loved me, too. I untied him and we went to bed and continued making love. I'm pretty sure Mia was conceived that night at the Plaza.

The next day he was shooting up again, and we had a huge fight. He tore up my clothes and stomped on my shoes. I went out and bought thousands of dollars' worth of new clothes and charged them all to his American Express card.

TEN
Great Expectations

As soon as we got together, Steven and I agreed that we were going to have children as soon as possible. "I want you to have my baby," was one of the first and most endearing things he ever said to me. As his drug use and violence increased, I somehow convinced myself that starting a family would set us on the road to normalcy.

Aerosmith's spring tour in 1978 took us through the South and ended in Florida. I was so eager to become pregnant, and Steven wanted it so, that in every town we'd stop at a drugstore and buy a home pregnancy kit, and I'd go in the bathroom of our hotel suite and test myself. By the end of April I hadn't had my period, and the tests were turning up positive. Steven was so excited that he made me buy every single brand of testing kit, and we got positive results each time.

I went to a doctor in Memphis, and he took a blood sample and told me to call him in three days. I phoned him from our hotel in Florida, and he said I was definitely pregnant. I told Steven what the doctor said, and he proposed to me that same day.

I can't even remember what hotel we were in at the time—that's what being on the road is like. But how it happened I will never forget. It was in the evening, after a room-service dinner, and he asked me to sit in a chair. He got down on one knee and told me that I was the woman he wanted to spend the rest of his life with. He took out a little folded piece of paper and opened it. Inside was an old-fashioned diamond ring, with a marquise stone in the middle and two little pear-shaped diamonds on either side of it. He told me it had been his grandmother's. She had taken it off her finger as she lay dying in the hospital and told him to give it to the woman he was going to marry. I found out that Steven had someone get the ring out of his safe-deposit box in New Hampshire and send it to him, so apparently he was planning the proposal even before the pregnancy was confirmed by a doctor.

I was swept away on a nonchemical high, alternating between elation and doubt. There was no doubt that I loved Steven and that I wanted this baby. But I was also scared of what I was getting into.

Still, he'd proposed on one knee, like a gentleman, and it was so sweet. He was wearing jeans and an emerald-green silk shirt that I'd bought him, and I had on a flowered dress, a silk hippie peasant dress. He was laughing, and he gave me the reasons why he wanted me to marry him: I was a special woman to him, I hadn't been with everyone in town, he was very happy that I was pregnant, this was what he really wanted, and would I please marry him? I squealed, "Yes!" Then the two of us went and knocked on the doors of all the other band members and told them we were engaged. They were genuinely happy for both of us. Despite all the craziness, they wanted what was good for him, and I guess I filled the bill in their minds.

The ring was fresh on my hand, not even an hour old, when Steven announced he wanted to go for a swim, alone, in the pool. I was hurt. I thought this was supposed to be a romantic time, and he wasn't supposed to walk off like this. It wasn't as happy a moment as I thought it should have been. I was newly engaged, and he'd gone off swimming, and I was standing there jumping up and down, thinking, *I don't know what to do!* I went out into the hall and was still jumping up and down with my fists clenched from fright. Then I realized the baby might get hurt from all that jumping. I even started thinking I didn't want this baby, that I should throw myself down the stairs, do horrible things to my body. I was a mess.

After two hours, Steven returned to the room with scratches all over him, particularly on his neck and shoulders. His explanation was that there had been some girls in the pool, and they were all playing in the water, and "someone was standing on my shoulders and slipped off," and all this bullshit. Either it was true, which is a little hard to believe, or he was having sex with someone right after he proposed to me. There were always groupies at every hotel, lying in wait for someone, anyone, in the band. Steven was daring me not to believe his little story about the girls in the pool; I could only pray that things wouldn't get worse before the baby came.

Why did I accept the proposal, knowing what I knew about all the women he'd been with? I was in love with Steven, I was in it up to my eyes already, and I always thought it would change, that marriage would settle him down. I thought this was going to make him happy at last, and that I was finally going to have a family. I wanted a family. I wanted to have all the things I never had as a child.

We went back to New Hampshire after the tour was over, and Henry Smith's wife, Gail, sent me to a doctor at the hospital where my daughter would later be born. He was going to be my obstetrician, so the tests were run again just to make sure the doctor in Memphis had been right. Steven and I were over at Henry and Gail's house when the doctor called and asked to speak to me. He said, "Yes, you are pregnant." I got scared all over again, and Steven was so excited. There's a big difference between getting tested on the road and hearing it from a doctor everyone knows and trusts.

Steven would play little games with our unborn child. He would drum on my stomach—that was one of his favorite things—and he would read to the baby inside, *Alice in Wonderland*, things like that. He'd play classical music for the baby on the stereo, Beethoven and Tchaikovsky. And he was eating like a horse, he ate for all three of us. Sometimes he would be so healthy and wonderful and homelike, and other times he would do drugs, and he wouldn't be nice at all.

The first months of the pregnancy were the best time Steven and I had together. Until I started getting very large, which wasn't until the end of the summer, we had lots of sex, and I think that was the most faithful period, on his part, of our relationship. He loved performing oral sex. I called him the Cookie Monster because he called a woman's genital area her "cookie," and he loved to eat cookies. He was ordinarily kind of passive, but he loved giving head. He loved getting it, too, but then he'd jump on board and finish his meal himself. You know, I hate him for making me do this. I never thought I'd have to expose my personal and private life. It's no secret that I'm writing this book because my alimony settlement is $252.08 a week, from a guy who just sold his song publishing to Sony for something like $34 million. Excuse me for being resentful.

Now that I've gotten through that outburst, back to our domestic life. We were starting to live like a couple, bickering, making love, learning each other's habits, becoming really, really close. Before going on the road again in the summer of 1978, we had a month or so at the Gray House in New Hampshire. Steven would shower every night before going to bed, and then he'd take out his electric razor and shave. I always wondered why he did it at night instead of in the morning. I think it's a habit he got from his father, or else he was being considerate of me, if you get my drift.

He'd walk around while he was shaving. He'd do the same thing while he was brushing his teeth, which made me a little crazy. I can't stand someone walking around and brushing his teeth and talking to me at the same time. You stand at the sink, and you brush your teeth. And it would make him crazy if I brushed my teeth and rinsed by scooping water into my hands right from the faucet. I was supposed to use the little cup by the sink, the one that never got washed. He thought it was unspeakably disgusting that I used my hands, and he'd scream, "Use the glass! Use the glass!"

Another thing that upset him was when I put things away in the medicine cabinet. I didn't want the tooth-brushes, toothpaste, and combs all lying around the sink. I wanted them hidden. He wanted them all in a handy little cup right next to the sink. And he was very meticulous about squeezing the toothpaste from the bottom, while I would just squeeze it wherever. It's funny, but now I'm the way he wanted me to be back then. I practically use a rolling pin on the damn tube. Maybe we should get back together!

He also hated it if I talked to him while the water was running, because he couldn't hear me. Of course, I did it on purpose. I would deliberately say some-thing in a low voice while the water was running or while he was blow-drying his hair, just to make him mad. It was safe to tease and provoke him then, to get even with him for all the times he beat me, because now I was pregnant and a person to be treated with care and delicacy—or so I thought.

Steven was hoping the baby would be a boy. He kept talking about "my son." I hadn't been tested for the sex of the baby, and I just knew it was going to be a girl, although I was hoping it would be a boy for Steven's sake. Meanwhile, I was buying little girl's things and hiding them—little yellow crocheted dresses and stuff. Terry Hamilton went shopping with me in Boston and said I was out of my mind, spending thousands of dollars on baby girl clothes when I didn't know what it was going to be. I told her, "I know I'm having a girl. I don't know why. I just don't want to talk about it."

We were married on September 1, 1978, in Sunapee, New Hampshire. The day was beautiful, the sun was shining, and the ceremony took place on the mountainside.

Steven's aunt Phyllis was over at the family resort, tape recording groupies talking about their escapades with Steven on the road. It was a wedding gift that I would later be presented with. I wore a pastel green-and-white silk chiffon dress with flowers and ruffles. I bought Steven a suit at Gucci in Beverly Hills, cream silk, with a pale pink-and-gray striped shirt and beautiful summer suede shoes. He looked the best I had ever seen him, and I was very much in love!

Joe Perry showed up with Elissa. He looked gorgeous in brown leather pants and a pale blue vest. She had on a long black skirt and green top, but she was so skinny that nothing looked that great on her.

I recall thinking what it would have been like if it had been Joe instead of Steven that day. It was scary to think that, but I really had never had a cross word with Joe, and we got along so well. He was the first one in that organization with whom I had bonded. Earlier that day, Joe and I had been alone at Henry Smith's house, and we were talking about the day and its meaning to the world, and to us, and we looked at each other and finally gave in and kissed that forbidden kiss. My heart was doing flip-flops. God, I really wish we had explored each other more in those years. I still remember that kiss today. It was right out of a movie—"the love that can never be, but always was." Afterward I tidied up my makeup and went off to marry Steven Tyler.

Steven and I tied a ribbon around my engagement ring and left it temporarily at the bottom of the hill, under the tree where his grandfather was buried. Don't forget, this was the very ring that Grandpa had given Grandma, and she had given it to Steven to bestow on the woman of his dreams. Then we walked to the top of the hill, where everyone was assembled. I'd left my bridal bouquet down by the grave (what an omen!), but Steven's mother graciously gave me the huge bunch of flowers she had been picking in the vicinity, so I carried in my arm a lovely collection of long-stemmed wildflowers.

Terry Hamilton was my matron of honor, and Augie Mazella, Steven's cousin, was his best man. During the ceremony, everyone was crying tears of joy—no kidding—and looking at Steven and me looking at each other. There were petals scattered all over the ground, and local police plus a private security squad at the bottom of the hill to keep kids away. Steven's father played the accordion. The ceremony was nondenominational and the vows were not traditional; they said something about two pillars needing to hold up a building (from Kahlil Gibran, I believe, or one of those Hallmark writers). We made sure to claim our independence.

After the ceremony we went back and retrieved my ring from under Grandpa's watchful eye, and everyone trooped over to King Ridge, a big catering hall overlooking Kearsarge Mountain. We had a genuine New England seafood festival, with lobsters flown in from the Atlantic and champagne on every table. The band had been assembled from a bunch of jazz players whom Joe Baptista had known over the years, and they were great. People danced and ate until the evening, when things started to deteriorate. Drugs were rampant (there were strangers in the bathrooms shooting up), and I was getting nervous about losing this day to another drug orgy. Everyone else was either flying back to New York or driving to Boston. I was upset and wanted to leave, so a group of us went to the compound on the lake, where Steven and I had been living in the Gray House. Soon Steven was nowhere to be found, and I was alone.

Brimstone, the drug dealer from hell, long since murdered, was one of the invited guests, and I figured if I found him, I'd find my new husband. Sure enough, they were down at the unfinished Big House, getting high. Then Steven came over to me with some bullshit story about Brimstone's girlfriend getting her finger caught in the electric railing that opened and closed the cupola of the new house, and they all had to take this wounded druggie to the hospital right away. I asked Steven to please stay with me, but no, he had to take Brimstone's chick to the ER. I'm sure they were going to party elsewhere. That was how my wedding day ended. Steven didn't show up again until early the next morning.

There was no honeymoon, figuratively or literally. Within a week of the wedding we were in Los Angeles, where Robert Stigwood was giving a big party for the premiere of *Sgt. Pepper,* and where I first became convinced that I'd made a terrible mistake.

I was almost seven months pregnant, but I was still able to have fun. I even wore heels, which Steven didn't like. I suppose he wanted me literally barefoot and pregnant. But I could still wear cute clothes, so I was a cute pregnant girl. Steven wasn't too keen on me even going to this event, but I had no intention of missing it. This was a big, elaborate Hollywood party. Everyone was there, tons of food and giant bouquets everywhere, and I was wearing a beautiful brown-and-gold antique silk-satin kimono top and velvet maternity pants. I must say I got a lot of compliments.

We were sitting at a round table, and Britt Ekland was standing over by a window. Steven looked at her, turned to me, and said, "Goddamn it, if you weren't here tonight I could probably be with Britt Ekland."

This was worse than a punch in the head. I was heartbroken. My husband had just announced to me that I, his pregnant wife, was getting in the way of his sex life. Britt Ekland? Rod Stewart had fucked her, and she was an important power-chick to fuck. It would have made Steven feel like he was "in." I guess that makes you a bigger star. It puts you on a higher level. It's climbing, pure and simple. Everything had a purpose. If you slept with a girl Rod Stewart had had, it made you more like Rod Stewart, though God only knows why you'd want to be like him. That's their whole thing, these "stars." It's like they actually want to fuck each other, but they use a woman as a go-between. It's always the same girl or one of a select few. She's got to be faintly groovy and presentable. It's a hetero-male thing, just another way they make fools of themselves. Some men are exceptions to this macho bullshit, and one of them is my dear friend Alice Cooper. I once brought Steven over to Alice's house on a previous trip to L.A., and Steven passed out on the pool table, so Alice wasn't crazy about the guy. That night at the Stigwood party, as I sat there stung to death by Steven's comment about Britt Ekland, I noticed Alice behind a huge potted plant. He was looking at our table. When Steven got up to cruise, Alice came over, walking on tiptoe, looking around to make sure Steven was gone. He sat down next to me, and we hugged, and we were so thrilled to see each other. He was my friend. He touched my stomach, and he made no secret of not wanting to say hello to Steven.

Soon after that I got tired and wanted to go home. My legs hurt, I couldn't stay up too late, and I had to sleep. Being pregnant is hard. Steven was furious. On the way back to the hotel, he was inhaling immense lines of coke and cursing me for being a drag on his social life. A few days later, at the St. Regis Hotel in New York, he smacked me really hard, the first time he'd hit me since our engagement. I remember standing by a window, where I'd hung some chimes, and I still can hear the sound of the chimes as I crashed into the window after he hit me. I thought I might have to run away to protect my child if he got really out of control. I was really in love with having this baby, I was so in love with her even before she was born. I felt so secure, so great. It was the most important time of my life, and I'd been stripped so bare by Steven that I started to focus my love on my child. It was a love affair going on within my own body.

By November I was too pregnant to travel, and from what I learned from Terry and Henry, the road at that time with Aerosmith was no place to be. Steven was occasionally passing out on stage or babbling meaninglessly to the crowd. The more sloppy the show, the more violent he was afterward, so I was advised to stay out of the picture. Also, Joe and Steven's drug habits had intensified their love/hate relationship to the point where they'd go at each other on stage, right in the middle of a show! They would actually draw blood in front of the audience. They were known not only by the crew, but throughout the music industry, as the Toxic Twins. Very attractive.

I still wanted to be at the band's most important shows, one of which was their return to the Spectrum in Philadelphia. At an Aerosmith concert in October of 1977, an M-80 firecracker was hurled at the stage by a "fan." The explosion severed an artery in Joe's arm and came close to blinding Steven. When we arrived at the Spectrum this time, for Aerosmith's November 25 concert, there were signs everywhere saying, "Welcome Aerosmith! We're Sorry! We Love You!"

I stood at the side of the stage, and it wasn't far into the show when things started flying out of the crowd. This was really wild, really dangerous. Joe Baptista rushed me off the stage into a dressing room, and I sat there listening to the muffled sound of the show, when suddenly the music stopped, and it got very quiet. I ran out to see what had happened. The guys were rushing off the stage, and Steven's face was covered with blood. A bottle had shattered right next to him, and glass splinters had hit him in the face and under his chin. I ran to Steven, and the band was deciding whether or not to go on with the show. I was not shy about voicing my thoughts, and the decision fell to Steven; he'd been the one injured, and he was the lead singer. I was saying, "What are they going to do, shoot him next? Fuck them! They don't know how to come to a show and behave. Why are you risking your lives?" I was always so afraid something just like this would happen to Steven, and when it came to really personal stuff, he would listen to me.

The road manager said, "Well, Steven?" Steven
looked up at me and said, "I don't think so." We were
out of there in a minute, well before the audience
knew the show was over for good.

It was decided that I would spend the last month
of my pregnancy at home in New Hampshire.

ELEVEN
Rock and Roll Mom and Dad

Steven's earliest attempts at being Daddy were sort of adorable, alas. In the last month of my pregnancy, he was there for me a lot, and he became increasingly agitated. He insisted I eat everything in sight, I needed to "feed the two of us," all that stuff: "Have some more strawberries, milkshakes, french fries!" Earlier in the pregnancy he'd been eating for the three of us, but now his attention was focused on mother and impending child. I thought he was going to be a great father. I really thought I'd done something good for this man and for myself.

I had a healthy pregnancy, but there were always these backaches and pains. It's not your normal life. Steven, the big rock-and-roll star, had a plane on standby in case it was needed when the baby started coming. A plane? To take me where? There was a perfectly good hospital down the highway, but these fucking rock-and-roll stars are the worst assholes when it comes to this. The world has to know that a plane to nowhere is available for the arrival of this tiny extension of themselves.

Steven was with me when I started going into labor, and he was very diligent, I have to say. He wrote down the time of the contractions on a piece of paper, and he was getting nervous. More nervous than I was, because I went to sleep while he stayed awake. All of a sudden I woke up, and I was freaking out. My body was going to have a baby. Uh oh. It wasn't like anything else I had ever felt. I thought I was literally going to die. I wanted to die. I wanted to stop the movie, please, right here, let's just think about this for a while. I was on my knees, crawling to the bathroom, because I couldn't get off the floor, and I had to brush my teeth because I knew I was going to the hospital. I was lying on the bathroom floor trying to reach a toothbrush, and Steven was just bouncing off the walls. He was thinking rationally enough to call the doctor, who told us to get to the hospital right away, and I was begging him to make it stop.

I'll never forget the look on his face. He didn't know what to do. His eyes were bugging out of his head. He was pale as a ghost. I needed socks, and he put socks on me, but my skin was too sensitive and it felt like steel wool on an open wound, so he had to take them off. I found myself going through some strange behavior, like pulling blankets around me to make some kind of nest. It was really uncivilized. You think abortions are ugly? Just having a baby is too freaky for me.

We had a Jeep and a Porsche. I was not getting

into any Porsche. He got me into the back of the Jeep, which had been prepared in advance with quilts and strange little items like lemon drops. He was helping me, and that was absolutely wonderful despite all the pain and horror.

My skin was burning and I wanted him to hurry up, then slow down, then hurry up, then slow down, and the poor guy was going nuts, driving down the highway with me yelling at him from the back. We got to the hospital, and Steven made me walk inside in my enormous agony. The attendants rushed me into a wheelchair, and this nursey type says, "Hello, please don't have it right here." They're probably used to the women up there squatting, dropping the kid, chewing the thing off, and going back to picking apples or whatever they do.

I'm sorry, giving birth was not a beautiful experience. It was one of the worst things in my life. I forgot the breathing lessons. I wanted them to push the baby back up inside me. I wanted out. No painkillers. I was delirious, and Steven was trying to take photographs of this sacred moment. He got one shot of my poor legs spread open with a sheet over my crotch. It took me a couple of years of staring at this picture to figure out what it was. I guess it was taken just after the baby was born. I didn't scream, and the doctor was wonderful; he was the only one I could hear and the only one I trusted.

They told me the baby was a little girl, and Steven was taking pictures, and I was trying to smile. I didn't even feel the thrill, I was too exhausted, and you're so in love, it's disorienting. This is the most important day of your life.

And then all this other stuff came out of me, and I didn't want to look at it. I fell asleep and later woke to see Steven with the baby in his arms, on the phone with Tom Hamilton: "It's a girl! I have her in my arms! Oh God!" That was so sweet.

My in-laws were *so* helpful. We were in the hospital for two days when we started getting phone calls from fans! Steven's mother was giving out the phone number of the hospital! I guess her number is no secret from Aerosmith watchers, and she's telling them, "Oh yes, they're at the Mary Hitchcock Hospital. Here's the number, give them a ring and congratulate them!" "Hey man, this is Bob Jones from Indiana. I called your mom and she gave me your number. Far out, man!" So Steven had to ask his mother to cease and desist.

He and I started going through names for our new daughter. I had picked names like Scarlett and Zuni, after the Indian tribe. He wanted more traditional names like Rebecca and Sarah, nice biblical names, not that he knew they were biblical, they just sounded like sensible New England names to him. We argued constantly about a name. They told us we didn't have to pick a name for thirty days. Steven agreed, and we were going to leave the hospital with No Name Baby. But I put my foot down, as it were, and we were going to have a name on that birth certificate before we got out of there. So I named her Mia, because in Italian it means "mine," and her middle name is Abagale, and I spelled it that way just to be nontraditional. I think it was kind of a battle of the wills, but I knew I was going to win.

When we got back to the house, he wanted to put Mia into the extra bedroom, which we'd been decorating for a baby, but I insisted that she was going to sleep with me, and I got my way on that, too.

But all things got bad. Mia was born December 22, and we brought her home on December 24, Christmas Eve. He didn't give me one fucking Christmas present. When I was pregnant, I bought all these things for him, but now there was nothing for me. I had no nurse, nothing. I was supposed to go up and down the stairs, even though the doctors said I shouldn't, because there was no one to help. I needed a nurse, but Steven didn't believe in them. And he didn't want maids in the house. He thought I should do everything.

This was not why I had gotten married for the second time. I could barely walk, and here I was washing out little baby diapers, and I didn't know what the hell I was doing. A week later it was New Year's Eve, and Steven wanted to go to a party. So I had to take this newborn child to a party, and it was so icy out, and I was carrying this wrapped-up little thing, and I could barely walk indoors, much less on the ice, but he's got to see his goddamn friends on New Year's Eve, so it was a nightmare from day one.

The new year begins, I'm a new mom, I love my baby, and I hate everyone else in the world. I don't care about anybody, just this new little person, and everything was just groovy. Mia's father, meanwhile, was so immature. He wasn't a father, he's never been a father, he still isn't a father, he's a guy who had a kid. Physically. Of course, I wouldn't know, because I never really had a dad either, but he's not like the dads my friends had. He's there only when it's convenient for him.

Steven did change a few diapers, and he loved giving Mia a bath and taking a bath with her. He would do these wonderful things, and then he would let the babysitter go, because he decided we didn't need one, we could take the baby with us wherever we went. Then he started eating Mia's food. He loved it. Strained veal? He couldn't get enough of it. Sometimes there was none left for Mia.

He was jealous of the attention I was giving her, but I hear that's pretty common, so I won't blame him too heavily for that. On the other hand, he was using drugs around the baby all the time. One time he had done so much coke that he got paranoid and hid naked in the closet of Mia's room because this guy had come over whom he didn't want to see. Obviously, I didn't want him anywhere near her when he was that wigged. Another time, he was babysitting her when she was starting to walk. Later I noticed that her tiny pinky was all blue. "What's wrong with her?" I asked. He had passed out while he was supposed to be watching her, and she had been racing around the house and broke her finger. I knew better than to try and blame Steven, though, because he would have hit me if I'd said anything.

Here's another amazing anecdote. Mia was about two or three weeks old, and we were at someone's house, and everyone was stoned except me. I went upstairs to take a nap, and when I came down, my baby was sucking on this woman's tit! I could have killed them all! I can't say who the woman was, I don't want to get sued, but she was just letting Mia suck on her nipple while Steven sat there and watched.

I said, "Give me my baby," and I took Mia and went back upstairs. Steven followed me and started to explain that they were just having fun, and I lunged at him. I slapped him across the face and scratched him with all ten fingernails. Then I grabbed him by the shirt and told him that if he ever did anything to this baby, I would kill him. I had never before hit him without thinking I was going to get it back, but this was beyond my control. He apologized, and the woman later apologized, too, but you can't imagine how much I hated her from that moment on. It was the most vulgar, filthiest thing I had ever seen. And it turned out Steven and this woman had talked it over beforehand—"Gee, it must feel good to have your tit sucked by a baby." "Wanna try? Here."

He always remembered that incident. He told me I was like a mother cougar. Good, that's what I was, and that's what I wanted him to think I was. He went to spank her once—he wasn't even living with us then—because she'd picked up a toy squirt gun and aimed it at him. He yelled, "Don't you ever point that at anyone!" and moved toward her, and she cried,

"Mom!" and I just pulled her away and shouted, "Don't you ever touch her! No one is allowed to spank her but me."

That didn't mean I didn't get hit myself. Once, at the St. Regis, he punched me really hard while I was holding her. In 1981, after we moved from New Hampshire to New York, he grabbed me by the hair, threw me on the floor of our apartment, spit in my face, and kicked me while I was on the ground. She came out of her room, and I said, "Get back in your room," but she wouldn't go. Seeing her gave me the strength to push him off me. That's when I stopped wanting him around. It wasn't me getting beaten by him; it was having Mia see it happen.

I am fiercely protective of her. A delivery guy came to the house one time, and he was kind of looking at her, and I wanted to punch him in the head. I said, "What are you looking at?" In New York when she was eleven, she had boobs and men would look at her in the street, and I'd go, "What do you think you're doing? This is a child!" She's seventeen now as I write this. I've got to ease up a bit.

Steven has become this real sophisticated pop. Mia went down to Florida to visit him in 1995 and didn't tell me her boyfriend was going to be there, too. But Steven knew, and he booked a hotel room for the two of them. He never called to ask me if it was okay if my daughter and her boyfriend stayed in the same room. Let's face it, I can't stop them from doing what they're going to do, but I don't approve of it, and she is my child. And her father shouldn't be booking hotel rooms for her and her boyfriend. I'm old-fashioned that way.

As I write this, the old bastard has come back into our daughter's life in a most intrusive and unwelcome way. Suddenly he's interested in her education, and he's keen on finding her a boarding school, the kind where each girl has her own horse. I don't think Mia wants a horse, and I think that her friends tend not to be horsy types either—she's a little more Bohemian than that, a little more, shall we say, multicultural. But I know what Steven's agenda is: I can just imagine his accountant saying to him, "Listen, if she doesn't live at home, you don't have to pay the rent on her mother's apartment. Get the kid into a boarding school outside of New York, and your ex-wife can find herself a nice little studio apartment in Queens. You'll save thousands of dollars a year!"

This concept was undoubtedly one that Steven couldn't ignore, because suddenly he's pulling her out of school—without my permission, and I *am* her legal custodian—and driving around the countryside to such institutions as Miss Pritchard's School for Young Ladies, the two of them in the back of a limo, with him on a cell phone to his Higher Power, i.e., his lawyer, no doubt.

I intend to ignore whatever riding academy Steven comes up with. It's a little late to burst on the scene with all these plans for educating a child whom he's paid precious little attention to for the first seventeen and a half years of her life. My daughter will go to a fine school in New York and live at home with her mother, who has been her only real parent since the first weeks of her life.

When I first planned to do this book, I was going to give Mia a chapter of her own to write. What motivated me was a mixture of guilt (have I been fair to her?) and blatant curiosity (gee, I wonder what she saw when I wasn't there). Now, it doesn't make much sense. I think she might want to write her own book one day. But I have to take full responsibility for this one. There are no rebuttals here, no points of view other than mine. Besides, her father refuses to pay for a decent computer for her, so how is she going to write her chapter?

I do feel guilty about the mess I was during the early years of her life. Still, I rescued both of us from drug hell in New York in 1982, and I rescued us both again from New Hampshire hell eight years later. I was always a tigress of a mother, and Mia was never physically abused or hungry. Emotionally abused by me? I hope not, but I was a drug addict until she was almost four years old. I have a lot to answer for, I admit that.

Emotionally abused by her father? You bet. He has a lot more to answer for than I do. If Mia disagrees with that, she can go on every talk show in the world, and she can give interviews in every magazine that's read by her generation and mine. What the hell, she can move out, go live with a boyfriend (or whomever she chooses), get married. Don't get me wrong. I don't want her to move out. We're very close now, we understand each other, we're good roommates.

I've learned a lot about being a mother, and I am far
from always being successful at it. I like to think she
needs me, and I know I need her. Mia won't even ask
Steven for things, because she knows she won't get
them. It's such a sad thing. She wants a guitar. This
fucking guy will not give her a guitar. I told him we
had to stop piano lessons because we don't have a
piano in New York, so why don't you give her a
guitar? And he said, "Well, she just wants one because I have one." Well, that's a good reason! He
gets all this free equipment, and he can get anything
he wants. Mia asked this young musician we know if
he would give her a couple of guitar lessons. He came
to me and said he could not believe that Mia Tyler
came to *him* to teach her a few chords. He would
gladly do it, but he couldn't believe that she has ac-
cess to the greatest rock-and-roll stars, and she asks
him for a lesson.

He's just not there for Mia. The only time he's
there for his other daughter, Liv, is when she's on a
photo shoot. But he's there only for himself. Whenever he's in rehab he cries and feels guilty. He lives
a luxurious lifestyle, in the biggest house in a middle-
class neighborhood, so he looks like the big cheese.
He pays for school and that's it. Mia wants a Prada
dress, that's $700, and he won't buy one. You'd think
he'd want his daughter to be well-dressed so she can
hang out with the other rock kids. Why doesn't he
give her a credit card? I don't get it.

Here's a little tale to break hearts. It happened just
before Mia and I moved away from Steven and to

New York in 1982. Mia was three, and she and I were
visiting a friend of mine from Los Angeles who was
staying in a suite at the St. Moritz Hotel. The three
of us were in the bedroom, and in the living room
was one of those combination radio-TV setups they
have in hotels, and an Aerosmith song came on. Mia
started screaming "Daddy! Daddy!"

I never even knew that she knew "Daddy" all that
well, but she knew it was his voice, and she thought
he was coming to see her. I had to explain that it
wasn't Daddy, just his voice on the radio. My friend
and I both started crying; it broke our hearts. He
hadn't seen his daughter in so long. I called him and
said, "You've got to come and see her." And my
friend phoned him, too, and he said, "How dare you
speak to me about these things!"

There's been so much water under the bridge since
then.

Sometimes I still wish he was a drug addict so he'd
have an excuse for being the no-account father he is.
I think he's full of shit. I hate to say that. All he does
is talk about how he's trying to improve, and he puts
up this Hollywood facade that he's got going with
Liv. He talks to women like they're either little girls
or maids. He cannot talk to us one on one. I think
Mia is still waiting to have a daddy. I think she's
afraid he might die before she ever gets to know him.
I think she knows him as well as he'll ever know
himself. That's the kind of person he is. I learned I
can't prevent her from going through what I went
through. I'm constantly warning her about him, prob-

ably too much, perhaps to the point where she'll just tune me out and do something bad because she's been told how bad it is. I hope not. But she has a boyfriend who is very nurturing and very caring. He doesn't screw around on her; he's not wild. He's so gentle, and she seems to be happy in the relationship. She went out with these guys the other night, and one of them was a male model, and when she came home she told me, "Oh, one of these guys was so hot." She could have fooled around with him, but she chose not to. She told me that just experiencing that temptation made her realize how much she loved and cared for her boyfriend. She even said that to her father, and he just looked at her blankly, trying to absorb it all. He's almost fifty years old now, and he finally seems to be learning how to respect other people's boundaries. I criticize him a lot, but I support him in everything he does to make himself a better person.

In about 1994 Mia was interviewed on one of those entertainment tabloid TV shows and they asked her, "What do you think of your father's stage presence?"

Mia replied, "A forty-six-year-old man groping himself onstage? I think it's disgusting."

Her answer got picked up in *TV Guide* and she got three "cheers" and one "jeer" for what she said, and in *Rolling Stone* it was one of the quotes of the year. Steven saw the same show in Boston with Liv, and he refused to speak to Mia for three weeks. When he did, he told her he was pissed off that she had said that. He didn't scream or holler, he just told her he was pissed off. She told him she was just telling how she felt.

A DJ on WNEW played an Aerosmith song and was talking about Mia's comments regarding her father fondling himself onstage. "You know how some parents teach their kids lessons? It works the other way around in the Tyler clan!" I'm so proud of her healthy attitude. He's her father and she loves him, but she does not find him sexy. Thank God for that.

TWELVE
Newlywed Blues

The success of the Aerosmith album *Live Bootleg,* which went instant platinum (one million units sold) and got as high as number thirteen on the charts at the beginning of 1979, was heartening news for all of us. There was some touring, but mainly the guys were getting ready to record their next album, *A Night in the Ruts*, which was recorded at Media Sound in New York and came out at the end of the year. During the recording, we lived in a suite at the St. Regis.

There was a tour that summer, and I was on the road sporadically. Steven didn't want the baby on the road that much, and I couldn't stand being away from her for a second. There was a conflict. I wanted to be with him, because he would freak out if I wasn't there, but I also wanted to be with Mia. Of course I wanted a full troupe of English nannies, but there was no chance of that. I would join the group whenever Steven's begging got to be more than I could bear. The glamour of the road? I'll get to what there was of that later on, but being around Steven Tyler can take the glamour out of just about anything.

After Mia was born, our marriage irrevocably changed. It was like what had happened with my real father. The same thing was happening to me that had happened to my mother. I had Mia when I was twenty-six. My mother had me when she was twenty-six. The marriage was over by the time I was two, and the same happened with me and Steve. The good part, though, was that we managed to stay really tight. We were so compatible in some ways, so complementary, like salt and pepper. He's earthy, and there's an earthy element in me, too. I was extremely sophisticated compared to Steven, and he brought something into my life, you know, a get-down-and-smell-the-earth-and-eat-the-grass quality. But he was still too primitive for me, and I was much too sophisticated for him. I don't mean clothing and style stuff, but more intellectual things. To this day he even says to me, "You're too intellectual."

When it clicked, it clicked really well. When it was between Mia and the drugs, it was over. When there was no way he was going to stop, when his addiction got so pervasive, when the dark side took over, the relationship was over. We could dress compatibly, we were a striking couple, we were a good-looking couple, interesting, dynamic. He could make me laugh hysterically. He could imitate all the cartoon characters, like Sylvester and Foghorn Leghorn, and Curly of the Three Stooges, and I was just a sucker for guys who could do that, but not anymore. I would sit there and almost wet my pants. He would sing little songs for me; he would entertain me. He was a combination of a big brother and a boyfriend.

But when it was bad, it was horrible. He didn't like me wearing spandex disco pants; he thought they were too tight in the crotch. If I got too skinny, he didn't like it. He'd tell me to put more necklaces on to cover the bones. He knew what buttons to push more than I did. Steven would punch me in the head and say, "You deserved it. You pushed the wrong buttons." When I was quiet and more childlike, he seemed to like that, but he was so fucked up, one minute he loved you for doing something, and the next minute he couldn't stand you. To this day he resents it when I bring up the bad times, and he complains that I don't recall the good times, and to him the good times were buying me things and going shopping. For him, that was enough. I wasn't supposed to remember the black eyes; I was only supposed to remember that ring from his grandmother. I guess that's what that ring was for, to erase the bad times.

And he's never, ever apologized to me. After AA, when he got sober, he never apologized to me. (You're supposed to apologize—it's one of the fucking twelve steps.) Step off the pier, for all I care. In a way he's apologized to Mia. He would send her letters from rehab, but I never got any letters. Whether he feels guilty, I don't know. I don't think it would be polite of me to ask him to apologize. I'm trying now not to care how he feels.

During our marriage, when we should have been

growing together, we were shrinking, shrinking, shrinking, because of the drugs. I should have been becoming a woman, an adult, married with a child, and yet I was reverting further and further back into the safety net of being a child. It's only this past year that I've accepted the fact that I'm an adult. I acted immature around him, because I thought that was what he wanted, so I didn't know how to deal with anything.

Drugs destroyed Steven, me, and the band, all at different times, but with a certainty that no one looking back at it can deny. Okay, drugs are a symptom, not the disease; I'll buy that. We were disturbed people to begin with, and the relationships between us and among the members of Aerosmith were disturbed, too. But the drugs brought out everything with a vividness that was horrifying, life-threatening, catastrophic.

Steven made attempts at recovery while we were married, but they were lame. Once he had to write me a letter as part of his therapy, and I had to write him a letter that he was required to read out loud to his group. He actually called me to say I was sweet to put in my letter how afraid I was for him, and that I was afraid he would be angry at my honesty about the cocaine. This he thought was sweet; Mr. Nice Guy, who during our divorce said he didn't remember marrying me.

He checked into Hazelden, the famous rehab in Minnesota, in 1985, but drugs were smuggled to him while he was a patient there. When he got out, he continued abusing drugs. Teresa, who is now his wife, was in a hotel room nearby, waiting for him. Steven went to see his then-manager, David Krebs, and he was standing in the rain, begging David for money. David rolled up the window of his car and drove off, and that was the end for them. David had seen Steven collapse on stage in Portland, Maine, and that was when he knew it was over. He told me he looked at Teresa and saw the eyes of a rat. "I saw evil person-ified," he said, and I never heard a man describe a woman that way. "It's a look you see in rats' eyes." God, I've never heard anything like that in my life. Men look at women and they see boobs, they don't come up with moral judgments like that unless it's pretty extreme.

I've seen Steven collapse on stage myself. All of a sudden he'd be on the ground, not writhing around, but with his foot wiggling. I've seen him have sei-zures, too. At first I thought it was part of the act, and I thought, *Oh, this is new, this is dramatic, this is cool.* Then they'd be carrying him offstage and giving him oxygen, which was always at hand. He was al-ways so weak from the drug abuse.

I stopped going to shows completely after a few years of our marriage. I had been taking my life in my hands, because when he came offstage he would go crazy. He'd throw anything he could pick up at anything that was in his way, especially women. "You cunts, you fucking whores!" he'd shout. If I walked into the dressing room, I'd get thrown to the floor if I went anywhere near him or spoke one word to him.

He was crazed, wiped out, and violent. Whatever energy propelled him onstage turned evil after the show. Joe Baptista and the other guys were always trying to protect me from him. "Don't go back there," they'd say. It was a nightmare.

Of course, Steven's drug use would lead to canceled shows, and the other guys would be furious and totally helpless. "Oh shit, here we go again," they'd say. They're ready to do their jobs, they're out there to work, they've got their own problems, and they've probably gotten high, too. But Steven was way out of control from the inside out.

It took me a long time to give up hope for him. I thought he was so talented, a suffering poet. He would write the most beautiful love letters, the most beautiful poetry. And he'd draw ivy branches around the poems. It was all "You and me forever," very lyrical. That's the part I romanticized. And I still believe in it. I still have love/hate feelings toward him. I can't believe I was so wrong about him, and I can't believe he ever really stopped loving me. It's heartbreaking at times. Sometimes I break down and cry my eyes out over him. And sometimes I'm so consumed with loathing that I think I'm going to burst. I was in over my head. I mean, he's said publicly that when he was on drugs he would fuck a crack in the sidewalk. For nine years of my life that man was my husband.

On the other hand, there were a lot of incredible, fabulous, wonderful things in our lives. Most of them had to do with the love Steven and I had for each other, and with the huge amounts of money at our disposal. You can become very spoiled as the wife of a rich rock star. And I mean rich. In 1976 Aerosmith had its first million seller with the single "Dream On"—it had been rereleased following the success of the albums *Get Your Wings* and *Toys in the Attic*. The first time out, in 1973, "Dream On" went only to number fifty-nine on the *Billboard* charts; this time it climbed to number three. Even Aerosmith's debut album came back onto the charts. The group was selling albums by the millions, headlining arenas, and the money was pouring in.

I loved being married to a rock-and-roll star. I grew up listening to rock and roll, and this was a dream come true for me. I was still very young at the time—twenty-four—and I still had that passion in me. This was the height of our youth. I'd done a lot of things, and I was ready to go wild. And Steven was someone for whom I truly felt affection. I really adored him. He's like mold—he grows on you. He can be so charming and delightful, and so needy, in a good way.

We must have been spending hundreds of thousands of dollars on the road. Private jets, limos, hotel suites, jewelry, clothing, drugs. And hundreds of thousands on the drugs alone. There would be hundred-dollar bills in every pocket of everything we wore, in bathrobe pockets, shorts pockets, dresser tops, everywhere. There was a ridiculous amount of money just lying around. That was for the drug dealers. Everything else was charged, of course.

All the girls did during the day, I mean the girlfriends and wives of the band members, was shop. You could always tell when we were happy, because we'd be in a big city, with big malls and expensive stores. Dallas was fabulous, Houston was fabulous. Terry Hamilton knew where the best malls were, and we were divine together, though I must say she was a little more tight with her money than I was. I spent like there was no tomorrow. I'd see a pocketbook that cost $2000, and if I wanted it, price was no problem. But I liked to think of myself as a smart shopper, and if a bag was $2000, I'd want to know why. How many were made? What's the workmanship? This was one of the most delightful times of my life— having the freedom to express myself shopping. No more rummaging through thrift shops for salvageable bargains. In fact, when you're newly rich, you're sus- picious of bargains. Only the born-rich and the poor go crazy for bargains. I was obviously neither at that point.

It goes without saying that we took limos from the hotels to the malls. The soles of our shoes barely ever scraped the pavement. I read that the Duchess of Windsor used to have her servants polish the bottoms of her shoes. Well, ours never needed polishing. I wonder how much trudging around the duchess had to do.

Oh, shoes, they were a special treat. We'd buy them in massive quantities. There was a place on Ro- deo Drive called the Right Bank Shoe Store. They'd close the door and lower the blinds whenever I came in. I'd sit there and drink wine; I could even get

stoned, they didn't care. I was buying a dozen pair of
shoes at $400 a pop. No, there was never a scene like
in *Pretty Woman* when Julia Roberts looks too slutty
to get served in a Beverly Hills store. Store owners
are smarter than that. You get on the route, and they
know who you are, or you go with someone who's
known to them. "Hello, darling!" and down come the
blinds. The sales help are usually all queens, which
makes it extra fun. "Oh my dear, I wish I could wear
that myself!" He probably has.

I had so much jewelry, beautiful stuff; Steven gave
me so much. I wish I knew what happened to it all.
One time Steven and I were in a hotel, and we were
fighting, and I thought he was going to kill me. The
bodyguards came and separated us into different
rooms, but I'd hidden all my rings and things under
the mattress of the first room. When I got back to the
room, everything was gone. There were good bodyguards and bad bodyguards, and the bad ones stole
everything. There was insurance, but sometimes I
bought so much stuff when we traveled that there
wasn't time to insure everything.

By the way, we learned from the bodyguards that
the guys were also shopping—for the girlfriends they
kept on the side. Like it was supposed to be some big
secret that they were fucking around. Please, just have
these bills paid, and do what you want. I didn't adore
the idea of my husband screwing other women, but
really, what could I do?

But when Steven and I made love, we did it everywhere: airplanes, hallways, hotel kitchens. That was

so much fun. I'm always asked if we ever had sex in
an elevator, like in the Aerosmith song. Sure, but I
wouldn't be so bold as to think the song is about me.
If he had sex with me in an elevator, he had it with
others, too. Sometimes I would listen to those songs
and think, *Whoa! That's interesting! I wonder who
that one is about?*

He'd buy me the most beautiful jewelry, and gold
to match my hair. On St. Martin Island he bought me
a Jamaican doll, a little black girl with a fruit basket
and a little hat and apron. And he said, "Look, she's
pregnant!" and I said, "Oh, how sweet," and he said,
"No, really look," and he had taped a jewel box under
her apron that had a ruby ring in it. When Steven
gave you a gift, it was always in a clever way. Or in
a sexy way, like that bracelet that was wrapped
around his cock that I mentioned earlier. He'd say,
"I'd love a bowl of cereal," and you'd go and get a
bowl, and there would be a jewel in it. Or you poured
out the milk, and clunk, a ring fell out. And I'd jump
up and down like a big baby. I had rubies and the
most beautiful diamonds. He loved to adorn me with
jewelry, and he never cared how much I spent on
clothes. He was always good about that. We had nick-
names for each other. I was Puna and he was Puma.
Back then it seemed cute; now I think it's pathetic.

I remember a pair of wonderful eighteen-carat gold
and coral earrings. The coral was very soft and it went
with my tan, and the gold matched my hair. If Steven
hurt me or made me cry, which he did a lot, he would
go and buy a bracelet or a ring. I had so many rings

on my fingers, because I could never decide which one to wear. I'd fall asleep with them on, and my hands would swell. I was like Ringo Starr.

When Steven was being kind, there was no one like him. Once I fell asleep on the plane, and I woke up feeling sick, and he had the vomit bag all ready. He must have been watching me. He'd brush my hair, he was very good at that, braiding it for me sometimes, and he'd groom me. He'd wake me up in the morning with a hot washcloth and wash my hands for me, like a baby.

We had a bond. It's what makes you want to stay in love, and it's what makes me love him to this day, even though I hate him so much at the same time. We loved each other so much. I was his little princess. Whenever he introduced me, he'd say, "This is my lady."

I loved the way Steven smelled. If someone smells good, it turns you on more, and Steven smelled fantastic. He had a warm, natural kind of patchouli scent about him: I wouldn't want him to wash sometimes, because his natural scent was so fragrant. They say Napoleon didn't want Josephine to bathe for months while he was away, because her odor turned him on so much. Well, months wouldn't go by for us, but I did ask Steven not to bathe for two weeks, except for an occasional sponge bath on his personal parts, of course. Sometimes his smell was the only thing that kept me from hating him. There was something chemical about it that made me forgive and forget everything bad.

To this day, though I'm legally at war with Steven, and I have so many reasons to hate him, if I get too close to him and I get that smell, I just become totally vulnerable, and I'm overcome with compassion for him. All the anger and all the reality of what he's done to me melt away, and his power over me returns. It's a power that no one else has ever had, and no one ever will have. He's just got this delicious poison that surrounds him, this divine, deadly poison.

Sexually, Steven was kind of passive/aggressive. You know, take me, ravage me, play with me. He liked to be taken, he wanted everything done for him and to him, he wanted to just stand there. But I never heard him say anything about finding another guy attractive, and I never saw him giving another guy the once-over that fags do—a look I know very well. Steven was once spotted buying a dildo at this sex store, but it was probably for one of his girlfriends, because when you're on a lot of cocaine you can't get it hard, and girls do need to be satisfied somehow.

When I heard about that, I was curious about what size dildo he was buying and whether it was the same size as his cock. I always thought he had just about the right size cock, for me, anyhow. I turned down a guy once because his penis was too big, and I thought it would hurt me. I asked him if he had a license to carry that thing. He was pretty good-natured about it. Some women like huge dicks, because I guess they're all stretched out inside and they need to know there's something in there. And fags are obsessed with cock size, because they're penis-happy. Men are so different from women in what they want; they think they've got to stick it in somewhere to believe that something has happened. I always found it vulgar to talk about a sexual encounter as just a sexual encounter.

I do like to watch guys jerk off, though. In fact, every guy I've ever been with sexually, at one time or another, I've asked to come outside of me so I could watch. It's so exciting to look into their eyes while they're coming; it's just fascinating, like that time with David Bowie. God, my daughter is going to read this and think I'm kinky, but everything I hear about what her generation does when it comes to novel approaches to sex leaves us grown-ups in the dust. I mean, I don't have a penis, and I love being with men and seeing it come in spurts. I've never seen semen hit the wall. I'd be interested in that.

I'd say that 15 percent of sex is the pure sex part, and 85 percent is affection, ambiance, tenderness, warmth, friendliness, fondness, cuddling, and something that clicks, like chemistry. And you thought I was a sex object. I hope you know by now that I'm not a sex fiend. Fifteen percent, that's the amount of a tip in a restaurant.

For every bad thing, Steven would try to do something good, shallow though it was. Sometimes he'd just pick a flower and hand it to me as we walked down the street.

He looks at photographs of me dressed as Marie Antoinette for a costume ball and he becomes mesmerized. He loves that clothing, that period, and his

obsession triggered him to write "Kings and Queens."
I showed him stills from the movie *Farinelli* and he
asked me if I was fantasizing about *him*, as if he were
something from the eighteenth century.

The last time he came to my apartment, he was
with his wife, and she's very nice. I don't hate her, I
pity her. She went right into Mia's room to visit with
her. Someone had just sent over some roses, and I
went into the kitchen to cut the stems. Steven came
in after me. I asked, "What do you want?" He said,
"I'm really hungry." I said, "There's food in the refrigerator," and then he got really close behind me,
like in my hair, and I repeated, "What do you want?"
and he said, "I'm just sniffing around." I took the
knife I was cutting the roses with and turned around.
"Take twelve steps back," I said.

He laughed at me and my "attitude." But when I
turned back around, he came up behind me again, so
I took the heel of my shoe and scraped it right down
the shin of his leg and drew blood. I felt like a mare
defending herself against a stallion, so primitive. Will
that be us forever?

THIRTEEN
Bustup on the Road

Security is a big word in rock-and-roll touring, and of course it doesn't mean financial security or emotional security or airport security, but strong-arm stuff, the protection from harm, fans, the press, anyone or anything potentially bothersome.

We had bodyguards galore, as in a security company that provided armies of bodyguards. The more drugs a group uses, the more "security" they're likely to have. As we all know, Aerosmith had a reputation for using lots of drugs. First of all, they needed the bodyguards for insulation from nuisances like the police and hotel managers who might have a problem with funny smells, behavior, and visitors. Additionally, the more drugs you use, the more paranoid you get, and the more convinced you become that you always need more and more security.

Isn't it odd that only one rock star, John Lennon, has ever been "assassinated," considering how many performers think it's an imminent threat? I'm surprised more musicians haven't been killed by other

members of their own bands, or their wives, the way
Gail Pappalardi shot her husband Felix in the neck.
There is logic in that. But musicians are not logical,
as a rule, and their wives tend to lose certain amounts
of emotional and mental clarity, too.

Also, the more sex a group has, the more bodyguards are wanted, because they also procure. During
a show, the girls who are eager to get laid work themselves to the front of the crowd and they take off their
blouses. The guys in the band are up there singing
and playing and, of course, checking out the hooters
dancing in front of them. When they see someone
who looks especially tasty, they work their way over
to the side of the stage and get the word to one of
the bodyguards. This all happens in a split second.
Then the bodyguards pass the word to the security
people who are working the crowd, who extract the
delicacy from the audience to backstage. Little do the
girls know that they may have to do the bodyguards
and the road crew before they get to any of the God-
like band members. Often the way of a groupie to a
band member will go like this: Once backstage, the
status of the piece of meat will be conveyed to the
crew: "I'd like a closer look," or "That one definitely," or "Try her out and let me know," are some
of the messages that get passed around between the
band and their loyal employees.

Each band member had a different type of girl they
liked. Joe liked really dorky, bitchy women. Sometimes I even thought he was flaunting the really trashy
groupies to upset me. These were really bargain-

basement broads. High-class chicks were not the ones coming around; these ladies were fleabags. And when the wives weren't around, the guys were fucking them like no tomorrow. I witnessed this action because I went on the road everywhere, thinking I was supposed to be with Steven—unlike the other wives, who only went to the major cities.

Throughout our tours, my friend Elissa Perry continued to be a handful. She loved to torture the airline stewardesses by screaming, calling them names, demanding things immediately. If they were starting with the carts for food or beverage service, she'd ask them to move them so she could get to the bathroom, *now*. And if they hesitated, she would stand there and throw things. It was insanity. I never saw anybody behave this way in my life, and Joe did nothing. He just sat there. Getting no response, she'd turn to him and beg, "Joe, Joe, you're not helping me!" He would have to defend her, because if he didn't, she screamed even more. "She's in my way!" And there would be all these people coming up, and the rest of us would be cowering in our seats. For the people who didn't know us, they could only sit with their mouths hanging open. There was never a plane ride when she didn't torture the attendants.

During Aerosmith's "Mudstock" tour in England in 1976, Joe called and told me about some of the tortures that he had to endure while they were married. This was during the year that I was married to David Johansen. At the time, Steven was having a short-lived affair with Bebe Buell Shivers, the mother of Liv Tyler.

They were at a big record company party, some guys from Queen were there, and Elissa, as usual, ordered everything on the menu—everything. There were a lot of music people there, and it was Aerosmith's first time in the U.K., and they were trying to make their mark. The waiter, a proper English gentleman, brought out the tray with all the food she ordered. She yelled, "What is this? I don't want any of this!" and she pushed the tray back into the waiter's face. Poor man! There he was with spaghetti on his head, scallops in his pocket. People just sat there, awestruck, asking themselves, *Is she having a sugar attack? Is she going into some kind of rage?* Joe told me he just sat there while people wiped it up.

She could be a very funny, loving person, but she had this side to her that was just insanity, spoiled rotten. She and Joe eventually lost their house in Newton, and divorced. The last I heard, she was living in California with their son Adrian, who is about sixteen.

In one *Aerosmith* book, the author reported that there was a feud between Elissa and me. As far as I know, there is no feud. Elissa was wild; she fought with everyone. She had been my best friend until I started seeing Steven, and then she went ballistic. I didn't care. I wasn't interested in that kind of action; it was not what I thought was cool.

Back to the touring days: Usually, after a show, the

other guys would get their women and leave. No one
wanted to hang out with Steven and me. Joey Kramer,
once he got married, sort of reformed; before that, he
was doing it in the parking lot next to his car. And I
really can't speak about Brad Whitford; I just don't
know what he was up to. His ex-wife Laurie probably
hates me; I didn't know her very well, but when I
was pregnant, I had this girl Karen Lesser come on
the road to help me out with morning sickness and
stuff, and she ended up marrying Brad.

A word about the "wife-swapping" tales that have
made the rounds: That would have been exciting, and
these guys were not exciting in that way. Their excitement came from their weirdness, from the black-
ness of their souls. Because they weren't really having
a good time. They were not wife-swapping. Steven
probably would have liked to screw Terry Hamilton.
I saw him put his hands on her breasts a few times.
I liked Terry, and she and Tom are still together.

The other guys in the band were obnoxious to Tom.
They used to call him the White Reverend White,
because he was such a WASPy guy. He came from
a country-club kind of family who made Ruger guns.
I think that bugged Steven; if Tom made a mistake
onstage, Steven would just go crazy. He'd complain
that Tom didn't have it together. I never saw anyone
complain that much about another person. "You
missed a note! You did it wrong!" Christ, it's only
rock and roll.

We had big, bossy bodyguards who walked around
like giants, protecting us skinny little things from the

big, scary world out there. Many times I had to call on one of them to protect me from my skinny little husband; and in fact, the security staff often broke up fights within the band before they escalated into something horrible, like a sprained finger, or anything that would jeopardize a concert from going on as scheduled. Really, their main job ended up being as babysitters for a bunch of unruly, spoiled brats who were dangerous to each other.

There was technically supposed to be one body-guard for each member of the band, but Steven had a few, because he was the most important person and the one most likely to get himself into trouble. Some-times they'd have to pull him off me in hotel rooms and backstage so he wouldn't kill me. If the body-guard wasn't there I'd have to call for him, or have someone else call down, and up they'd come to pull him away before he killed me.

Like the road crew, the bodyguards became family members. I really grew fond of some of them, like Mark, who was a huge, bearded giant. He had a won-derful girlfriend, so he loved to escort me shopping because then he could buy things for her. I would always buy him a shirt or something and charge it to the band. I don't think Steven ever knew. I'd say, "Hey, that would look cute on you, let me get it for you, what else do you need?" I was generous and easier to take care of than Steven and other members of the band, so I was a plum assignment.

Steven would be off looking for drugs and "poon-tang." Some of the bodyguards felt uncomfortable accompanying him on those missions. I think they felt bad for me, knowing what he was doing. "I'm not going to tell him what you do," one said, "and I'm not going to tell you what he does." Which was a signal to me that he was screwing around, because I clearly was not. So I started to think that maybe I should go looking for cute boys and have some fun on the road like the guys did, though I never did.

I've always hated backstage, even though for many people, especially ones who can't be there, it's rock-and-roll heaven. To me it's always been a lot of wires and ropes and technicians, lonely, unexciting, bad sound with a lousy view of the show. And there were never any cute people back there, only groupies who were fucking the road crew who thought they had made the A-list, nerds from the record company, and local radio station types who live for this supposed "VIP status." Not me.

Fortunately, Steven wanted me to be out "in the house" because he trusted my taste and my ears, and he knew I would tell them how the band sounded. Your sound technicians are always going to tell you, "It sounded great!" because it's their job to make you sound great, and they're terrified of losing control of the sound. Also, they stay in one place, at the sound board, and the sound is different all over an arena, and bands really do care how they sound in the worst seats. It's good business to care about that, because those are usually the youngest fans with the least amount of money, and they'll be back the next few times you come to town. The people with the best seats will be on to the Next New Thing, or too old to rock and roll in a couple of years.

So during sound check, before the show, when the house was empty, I'd listen from a bunch of different places in the arena and report back to Steven. Then I'd do it again during the real show, because the sound changes when the room is full of bodies, and the band played differently in front of an audience than they did during the check. Steven didn't like me to go out into the audience without a bodyguard, but I'm pretty slick, and I learned how to slip out the door. Just don't lose that laminated pass, because no one gets back in, and the local security people, usually off-duty policemen, don't know you from a hole in the wall.

As I wanted to make perfectly clear, I wasn't having sex in the bleachers or giving blowjobs to teenage boys, but it was fun to be around them. And these were real working-class kids, this was their big night out, and they were so rock and roll, pushing to get close to the stage. Steven used to ask me why there were so many guys up front. He wanted to see tits. That asshole. I'd say, look, they're proletarian kids, and here come hard-rock musicians who all the girls are going wild for, and these guys want to be a part of it. They want to see what it is. Do they want to be president of the United States? No. They're not getting laid that night, these are young boys, they can't afford to bring a date. This is for them.

Sometimes Terry Hamilton would come with me, and we'd go around the stands and check out the T-shirt vendors and the bootleggers, just kind of snoop around and see what kind of merchandise was there that the band wasn't making any money on, and report back to the bosses. There's no way you're going to have a sexual encounter during a show. It's really more fun just to stand around and talk to the fans. They don't know who you are, or God forbid they do, and you watch their faces and they're so excited they can't breathe. That's sexy. It's better than actual sex. I was turning some kid on to something that was his dream, and I was this fabulous-looking woman. And I could always kiss them if they didn't know who I was. I also always had cocaine in my pocket. How could I not? If I didn't, I was miserable. Anyhow, they didn't know who I was, and even if they did, who would they tell? Who would believe them? Is the boy going to call the newspaper? The only people who did that were the girls on the roadies' bus. Sometimes that would be a nightmare. Those roadies didn't give a shit. They got no glory, only some ass, and they banged it every which way. We were always hearing stories that some roadie stuck something unsuitable up a girl, in which case the police were called and charges filed.

The roadies' buses were completely off limits for the wives of the band members. I mean, this was *infra dig*, big time. But they have these incredible buses, little cities on wheels, and the drivers are very proud of their rigs, and they'd say, "You should come and look at the bus." They were incredible. TVs, VCRs, CD players, all this technology that was really up-to-date at the time. So, once I accepted the invitation and went to look at the bus. The roadies were panic-stricken. Here was the boss's wife, and I'm the only female on the bus. I'm going, "Hi, how are you all doing?" and inspecting the bathrooms, showers, kitchen facilities, like the queen looking over a new housing project or something.

Steven found out and he had a cow. He screamed, "Don't you ever walk on that bus again! It's not right! You're my wife!" And I'm like, "Jesus, calm down, I wanted to see what it looked like. They had all these cool video games and stuff."

But he knew what really went on after the shows, and I don't blame him for wanting me to be as far from that as possible. As I've said, there are these girls out there who are so desperate to meet the guys in the band that they'll go through the entire crew in hopes of actually getting to a musician. They had wild sex orgies, and they'd pass women around and use broomsticks and bottles, and it was all very degrading.

Not that Steven thought I was going to take part in any of this, but it was the vibe that disturbed him. I, the queen of the hive, had descended among the lowest of the low. I mean, these people don't even stay in the same hotel, because once they start thinking they can hang out with you, they don't work the same. You don't have the hired help sit down to dinner with you.

Hanging out in the audience was fun. At the time my whole kick was to feel young. I knew that I'd get my head smashed after the show anyway, because Steven was so violent. So I tried to catch some fun before the bashing began. I'd go out and jump around and dance, or I would sit at the sound booth and watch the show, put the headphones on and listen to it that way. I was part of a rock 'n' roll show, instead of flying in and flying out.

When Steven was on, it was magic. He had tens of thousands of people swaying with him, moving with him. He commanded them physically through his sheer energy. But after the drugs took over, he was too weak to do anything, and it was pathetic to watch him.

Sometimes you just have to say things. When he'd say, "Oh, I don't want to go out there, I don't want to do it," or Joe Perry would say, "I don't want to do 'Dream On' one more fucking time," I'd say, "Honey, that's why the kids are here. They want to hear 'Dream On.' You don't do 'Dream On,' you might as well just go home. Who do you think you guys are?"

I'm sure the Stones didn't want to do "Satisfaction" one hundred million times, but they knew they had to. Of course, bands get tired of doing the same songs, but those are the songs that made them stars, so they have to live with them. I can think of more heinous curses than having to perform a song that made a band millions of dollars for the thousandth time. I guess they read about Mick Jagger saying, "I don't ant to be doing 'Satisfaction' when I'm fifty." Meanwhile, he certainly is. But that they had said it because of Mick Jagger, or whoever, isn't the point. The point is that they weren't ready to go out there and give a performance that was worth the ticket price. And to me this was maddening. I grew up a real rock-and-roll kid and my fantasy had always been that these performers *really* believed in what they were doing.

Steven got to the point where instead of using the mike as this great prop that he waved around and spun like a baton, he leaned on it like a crutch. That sight made me sick, and then he would come offstage crying and screaming, "I don't want to do this!" and I'd say, "Well then, don't do it." And then he'd beat the shit out of me. He was lying to his fans. Here they were, their hands were up in the air, they were there for Aerosmith 100 percent, and the band was just going through the motions. *Get the fuck off the stage, then*, I wanted to say, *go away, you're a liar*.

Steven needed to hear that stuff whether he wanted to hear it or not. And to this day, it's difficult. He is surrounded by "yes" people. All these little slaves and minions. By talking to him I was trying to wake him up—*Steven Tyler, hello, do you know what you're doing?*—because I loved him, and I loved rock and roll. It had saved me, and had been my way of life since I was a little girl. But watching Steven and Aerosmith woke me up and dashed the fantasy. This is not to say that it was always like that. Aerosmith was one of the very greatest American bands. When they clicked, they were hot.

Steven's rapport with the audience was amazing.

He tells me now that the only time he feels really
alive is when he's on stage. So, he must have felt
guilty those years when he was performing behind all
those drugs, so sloppily. I've often thought that guilt
could have been behind the mad explosions of anger
after the show.

Living on the road was so unpredictable. Sometimes audiences were dead. I remember one show in
Poughkeepsie where we all wondered if these people
were alive. Were they humans or life-sized dummies?
Yet at other times they would arrive at a show and
the crowd would go wild. They were so receptive,
and the energy was phenomenal. Twenty thousand
people ready to rock, and sitting and watching the
lights come up, the music begin, and the curtain go
back, was so exciting. Aerosmith used to play the
theme from *Psycho* just before the show, and that
combined with the screaming still gives me butterflies
in my stomach. Often, just before a show, Steven and
I would stand holding hands at the bottom of the staircase leading to the stage. Once he was on stage, the
music began. The sounds of the guitar always made
me feel like a kid. And, boom! The curtain rolled
back and Steven's there with the mike in his hands.
This is when the power really began. There was so
much adrenaline pumping. It's as if something were
about to explode.

One time when I was watching the show from the
side, Steven ran over, picked me up, and carried me
across the stage. I'd never known my husband was
so strong; he's five feet ten inches and weighed only

about 140 pounds. I happened to be dressed fabulously that night, so I didn't mind being a spectacle, but I was worried I would be dropped. All I could say was, "Please don't drop me." I was wearing this beautiful black crocheted and fringed hippie dress with a body stocking underneath and black satin Givenchy boots. Stunning, with slightly sparkling stockings, so it was just perfect. And here we are, dancing on air with all the noise, and the guitars screaming, and still he could hear me perfectly when I whispered to him not to drop me. All of it happened very quickly, but it felt like we were in a dream in slow motion, like a car crash.

After the show, on the rare occasions when Steven wasn't throwing a fit, he'd listen to the cassette from the soundboard. If he asked, I always told him what I thought of the show. I think he appreciated my input and trusted me implicitly. There were times when we both agreed it was a good show. Then there were times he wouldn't be quite sure. If I was out in the audience, I would tell him what I thought. If I thought it was good and he didn't, I would say, "Don't worry, it was great, the vibes were great, it sounded great." And he always looked really pleased to hear that, and I loved those moments. It was such a treat for me to be able to make him happy. To see him happy in his work was the most important thing to me. But Steven was the type of man who dismissed positive stuff. Everything could have been great, but he was so tortured. Nothing was okay.

If I were to give you a ratio of how many times it

was okay after a show and how many times it was hell, I'd say it was okay one out of ten times. And by 1982, it wasn't worth taking a chance on being around Steven Tyler when the show was over. He was just too crazy.

Band wives always went to the show, and though I often sat in the audience, the others often stayed in the dressing room. One of my jobs was to prepare the food to take back to the hotel, because you couldn't get room service by the time we returned. So right before the last song, I'd go back to the catering table to gather some food, and there would be a fight over the turkey neck. Steven always wanted the turkey neck. Terry Hamilton wanted it, too, so I had to get there first to get it for Steven, or else there would be hell to pay. I also packed up Perrier, champagne, and the egg salad. Along with the obsession about turkey necks, the egg salad had to be a certain kind, a certain consistency, all of which was specified in the band's contract for the show. And in regard to the turkey, it had to be real turkey, absolutely no loaf, because he would hold it up to the light, and if he saw those freckles it would be all over the wall, and there would be tantrums and the egg salad might go flying as well. I mean, he was a psycho about turkeys, necks, and loafs. He had to see the whole turkey skeleton there before him, and no loaf next to it, and even then he had to inspect the meat. Don't ask me where this came from, and I never worked for Hormel, so I don't even know what a turkey loaf is. But Steven sure did; he was the living expert.

I wish I could remember how great it was on the road, but the memories are all clouded by Steven's psychotic behavior. There were so many times when everyone who could would get out of his way. It was hardest for me, because I was his wife. Where was there for me to go? He's a real textbook piece of work. He could be so kind, but then in an instant he could crack. What good was all the glamour of music and money when someone was punching you in the head at the end of the night?

And then there was the split between Joe Perry and Steven. It happened backstage at the World Series of Rock in Cleveland in the summer of 1979. That day, Elissa had walked by Terry Hamilton and threw ice cubes at her. Terry threw whatever she was holding at Elissa, *whoosh*, and Elissa went running up to the trailer, "Joe, Joe!" with this nasal voice no one could ever forget.

She went into the trailer to talk to Joe, but Steven was there and he and Joe began screaming. What had happened between Elissa and Terry wasn't really violent, or even really mean, it was so kindergarten, but she had made some demand on Joe as a result of this insult, and I guess it was finally too much for him. She had been pushing and pushing for him to get out of the band. She would say so all the time. It was very clear that was what she wanted, and he would do anything she wanted. She'd say to the others, "We don't need you," the *we* being Elissa and Joe. "We don't need to be in this band." And he would just stand there, would never tell her to just shut up. Elissa was always doing that. And Steven was very worried but angry at the same time. He would ask me, "What's wrong with her? Why is she doing this? What's going on? Why is this happening?"

People asked Terry to apologize to Elissa, but she wouldn't. So that was the final straw. I was standing outside of the trailer with Steven, and Joe said, "I'm out of the band." Later I remember Joe looking out of the window of the trailer at me and his expression seemed to say, *This is it, baby.* I could tell he was sad and frightened. It was horrific. I'll never forget that look. And then Steven came out and begged me to talk to Elissa. She wouldn't talk to me. I'd been trying to talk to her all along and all she could do was throw things at me, breaking glasses and bottles all over the place, even when I was pregnant. She was a lunatic. I had to protect myself from her as well as from Steven.

Boy, Aerosmith was such a trip. I felt like I was some kind of aristocrat hanging out with a band of gypsies; I had no idea of what made these people do what they did. But I didn't want the band to break up. I wanted us to get along like the guys in the Monkees.

Of course, the women got blamed for the breakup. Steven would say, "You cheap whores, you bitches, women are always behind the demise of every great band. Look at the Beatles!" Of course, this is total bullshit. As if Yoko and Linda and Patti broke up the Beatles! John and Paul broke up the Beatles! Steven and Joe broke up Aerosmith, and eventually, it was

Steven and Joe who put it back together. But blaming the women, really! *Bullshit*, I wanted to say. *This is between you guys, nobody else is on stage with you.* I always thought that was a really stupid cheap shot. This group was like Spinal Tap, exactly. It had become a caricature of a rock band. These guys were living out some fantasy, yet the music wasn't enough to hold them together. They were too fucked up.

Still, I felt badly for Steven. His relationship with Joe had been like a marriage which had turned into a horrible divorce. Two people who had worked, performed, and created together had now parted ways. I didn't know what Steven was going to do. Aerosmith was all he had. He was nothing without that band. "Coney Island Whitefish Boy" is about Joe Perry. I remember when he wrote the song, and couldn't think of a title. "Coney Island Whitefish" is the term used for the rubbers that you see floating down the Hudson, and I turned Steven on to this phrase, and so he named the song that, and it's definitely about Joe Perry.

FOURTEEN

Clothes and Boys

Steven Tyler became known for his court jester costume—a look that baffled me. Blowing rags? Please. Thank God that was one thing no one imitated. At Kiss concerts there are always kids in Kiss makeup, but over the years with Aerosmith I never saw one kid turn up at a show wearing Steven Tyler drag.

In any case, his onstage wardrobe was a very touchy subject. One time the rags he hung on the microphone weren't there. He was so flipped out that I had to make them on the spot. There I was, ripping fabric as he stormed around furiously because no one could find the box of rags. He was so out to lunch with everything he did. These were not rags for him. They were rags made especially for his mike. They had to be ripped and tied a certain way. It is so ridiculous how meticulous this guy was about those rags, especially the rags that were sewn to his pants. And let me tell you, this was not quality stuff. The clothes were made so terribly. A professional dressmaker would look at this crap and go, "Who made these?" Actually, he worked with the designers who made these costumes. He was very particular. He'd want them ripped and drawn on in a particular way that went with the stripe on the fingernail and with the teardrop.

The girls who worked with him as designers were these flaky hippie chicks without a brain between their ears, and they went on the road. They had their own rooms, their own airline tickets, and, before me, probably him. They were all his servants. He was always big on personal servants just for himself, but the only thing they had going for them was that they could sew.

Once we got together, I took care of his clothes after the show. It's actually hard for me to believe what I had to do with the stage clothes. They were full of sweat, which made them dry onto Steven. So I would first help him peel them off. Then I put them on, went into the shower, and washed them while on my body. According to Mr. Hoodoo Doctor Tyler, they couldn't be put into a washing machine, even if they were inside a pillowcase to protect them. After I got out of the shower I'd have to twist them, being careful not to twist them too much because that would stretch them. Plus, because they couldn't shrink, I had to tie a string around the ankle part, hang them up high, and use weights and ties so that they would dry just right.

And if I didn't do it properly, then he would have to do it, and believe me, this was no fun. Even with the costumes, Steven never felt right. When I wore bell-bottoms he'd say, "Why do you always look hipper and cooler than I do?," and I'd say, "Because what I wear I can wear on the street. It's a cool look. What you're doing is a costume." Then he'd get angry. I could never tell Steven he was wrong about anything.

Two years ago I went to an Aerosmith show and made friends with his new wife. I had never spoken to her before in my life. I think he's in love with her. He told me she had used "alternative ways" to get them drugs. "That's a *real* woman," he said. "How could I ever leave her after all she's done?"

When he was with me, I was above him—he couldn't keep up, but now he knows what kind of woman he needs. He needs someone to keep his shoes lined up in the closet. He's not this hip rocking guy who hires a maid to do these things. He comes from a very primitive type of background (Italian-Polish) where women stay in the house and cook.

He liked slaves, not servants. It's a different thing. When you hire a maid, you don't want to talk to her about anything other than what her job is, no small talk. But Steven would hire slutty chicks to work for him. He wouldn't hire real people.

I think Steven has a problem trying to make it into the upper-middle class, because he comes from a working-class, tract house, polyester kind of background. He tries to pretend he was born with a silver spoon in his mouth. (Actually, it was chrome!) And he's very envious of people who do things properly.

He'd visit someone who had actual servants and would freak out. He didn't want that. He didn't want me to have a proper housekeeper or a nanny or a cook. He wouldn't let me have a decorator when we moved into our first house. He said I should do it myself, like his mother did.

We had moved into the big house in New Hampshire in spring 1980, when Mia was still really small, just starting to walk. We were so excited to move in there. It was gradual; there was no grand ceremony. We decided that we were going to sleep there whether they were finished with the house or not to provoke those lazy workmen to get their asses moving. We had this big hospital bed that you could raise and lower that we'd bought while the house was still being constructed, and we had it moved in there so these "builders" would see that we were serious about wanting to occupy our new residence. It wasn't all their fault. Steven was often stoned, and he'd tell them to do one thing, then he'd do a five-foot line of coke across the beam upstairs and change his mind, so these guys' instructions were changing with Steven's moods. The house was still not done, and it was certainly not luxurious. I wanted a house full of sculptures and wanted to bring in a real decorator (someone from New York). Steven was absolutely against that; no way were those fags going to tell him how to live.

In early 1981 Steven and I were dividing our time between an apartment in New York on West End Avenue and New Hampshire on our complex. Mia was about two at the time, and we had various people working around the house. Steven finally realized that in a house this size, with a baby this size, I couldn't do everything. One of the housekeepers was a local redneck, Irish-Italian, I think, and she had a strong, strapping, sixteen-year-old redneck son who did yard work for us. He was a handsome boy, six feet tall, light sandy hair, blue eyes, sweet, strong, and athletic. He also had the biggest crush on me.

He always worked with his shirt off, and he had the most beautiful body. And he was strong! Once I saw him take both hands and grasp the spikes on the side of a telephone pole, lift himself up and extend his body out perpendicular to the pole. Imagine, here was a beautiful specimen hanging around, staring at me, flexing, and posing.

Now if my husband stood naked next to him, you would have a skinny thirty-year-old rock star who's been ravaged by drugs and a sixteen-year-old Adonis who maybe had drunk some beer. You can't blame me for making the comparison at the time, especially since I knew Steven was screwing around.

Once when Steven was out of town, I decided, *Goddamn, it's my turn to have some innocent fun.* I was really lonely and sad, and there was this kid. We were in the living room having drinks. He was wearing a T-shirt and jeans, and I was wearing some fabulous silk pajamas or something very un–New Hampshire. He went upstairs to do something, and he gave me that look. I thought, *Well, why not?* We went to my room, and I let him seduce me.

I saw this boy about three or four times after that. We used to make out like high school kids. He was sixteen and I was twenty-six, which was not so outrageous.

Once we went to my in-laws' house, because we thought it was vacant. We went upstairs to one of the rooms and we were doing it there, and his mother came home. The mother came in the bedroom, saw what was going on, turned around, and walked out. I don't know how she knew we were there, but needless to say it was not a pleasant scene.

Shortly afterward, Steven and I went to New York because he had some business with his managers. We had left Mia in New Hampshire with the housekeeper and her daughter. And lo and behold, this housekeeper went to New York and told Steven that I was sleeping with her son!

Of course, Steven freaked when he heard about it, and he immediately filed for divorce. He wouldn't talk to me. When I called the house to find out about my daughter, I learned that the housekeeper's daughter had taken my child and hidden her on a farm in Massachusetts with Steven's approval!

I was ready to kill them. I had to get lawyers. No one was on my side. Steven's family refused to help me, of course, even though they knew about his infidelities. In fact, they did everything to hurt me. Mia was brought from the mysterious farm in Massachusetts over to my in-laws' house in the custody of a court-appointed guardian. My lawyer arranged for me to go to the Tallarico house, because this was set up

to be a showdown. The housekeeper had been teach-
ing Mia to call her husband "Papa." Throughout this
time they'd been claiming that I was an adulterous
child molester whose baby didn't even know who her
mother was. So it was put into the hands of a guardian
to decide. But when I walked in the door and Mia
screamed out "Mommy!" it was all over. Naturally,
the guardian decided in my favor on the spot. I remember just looking at everybody as if I wanted to
kill them. They all disgusted me. I couldn't believe
this was the family I had married into.

Since Steven had filed for divorce, it was decided
that I would stay in the guest house with Mia when
Steven wasn't there, and that when he was home, he
would have Mia and the housekeeper and her daughter would take care of her. Eventually Steven and I
got back together, and the divorce talk was dropped
for the time being. Not long after this whole fiasco,
one day when Steven was taking a nap, the housekeeper came in and started working on some papers.

"Get out!" I said. "I work for your husband," she
said. "My husband works for me," I yelled. "Now get
out and don't ever come back."

She went running for Steven, but he said, "What
can I do? She's my wife." Then—he's such a weak-
ling—he said to me, "Maybe we should keep her
around. She does things." But I said, "She's outta'
here now, and her husband and her son. All of them,
out." And then the kid appealed to me, and I shouted
at him, "Get the fuck out of here! You told them
everything." He had told the lawyers every place we

had screwed—on the fox rug, in my bed, in the Porsche. I said, "You're a creep, you're a big mistake."

They took me to court, with statutory rape charges thrown in for good measure. It was kind of a joke, because sixteen is the legal age in New Hampshire, but they were desperate to get control of Steven and his money. Of course, they lost. The judge was John Jay Fairbanks. Two years later he was on "America's Most Wanted" for swindling elderly people. He committed suicide.

I was back in New Hampshire a few years after this, and I saw the boy, who was more gorgeous than ever, then twenty-one years old. Then I saw his mother, our beloved housekeeper, in a local restaurant. Her husband took her by the elbow and made her leave, as she was snarling at me. When they passed by, he asked, "How are you doing?"

I had had this fling because I was in a very sad place, and Steven was fucking everything that moved. So by this time, about five years later, I sent a message to Ronnie through his friends asking him to stop by the house. This was a calculated move made to infuriate the mother. We slept together three or four times, and though he wasn't as pretty, his body was bigger and stronger.

Still, it was a payback to his mother. *I'll just fuck your son again*, I thought. She had taken my child away. It was the least I could do. She eventually left town. Ronnie sent me all these cards from Florida, but when he came back I wouldn't talk to him. I'd done what I had to do.

And I certainly had learned a lesson about adultery with rednecks. My next extramarital flings would be with the country club boys, and not until several years later in 1984. I remembered them from years before when they were little kids on bicycles watching me. Suddenly they were all grown up, rich preppies with trust funds who went to boarding schools in Europe and driving their own cars. I'll refer to the one whom I had the affair with as "Freddy." I was at a restaurant near the lake in New Hampshire one morning and he and his friend were staring at me, so I gave them a little wave. They couldn't believe it. They came over and sat down, and soon we were hanging out.

My attempt to reconcile with Steven had ended with a disastrous trip to Hawaii in 1983, where his drug dealer was waiting for us at the airport. That should give you some idea of how well that little journey went. Anyhow, I was back in New Hampshire, thirty and miserable, and there were these adorable boys with pot, coke, big boats, and big cars. These boys were happening. And Freddy had long, blond hair and beautiful green eyes, like a semi-grown-up Luke Halpin, my first teen idol, or a young, pretty Robert Redford, or the Dutch Boy. He carried a flask of Scotch, and it was all very Gatsby-esque.

My houseboy was more muscular, because he had to work physically. This one just had to cash checks, so he was slimmer, and more fun. There was a gang of them, but I picked this one because he was the prettiest and most adventurous. He was into the Grateful Dead and Hendrix. He liked to wear a bandanna on his head with his long blond hair and pale green eyes. Finally, here was someone who was fun and cool and rich—he was not some primitive caveman like my out-to-lunch husband. I gave him his first blowjob, and told him he could come on my face. He was so thrilled. This was truly an adventure! I guess we fell asleep right afterward, because when I woke up I couldn't open my eyes. His preppy little load of cum had solidified and sealed them tightly shut.

This was a healthy kid, ripe for molding. We had a blast, but I did make him a little crazy. I became demanding, and he wanted to hang out with his friends. I was a spoiled girl, and I wanted my play toy all to myself. Then I said I wouldn't see him anymore, and he threatened to kill himself. He put a gun to his head and said, "The only way you'll get rid of me is if I die." What drama!

I said, "Then please go do it somewhere else. This is ridiculous. You're acting like a child." And he'd sit there and cry, then leave, then come back and scream, "Let me in! Let me in!" I had to lock all the doors and windows and go, "Please, go find your friends. That's what you should be doing. We can't be together, I'm a mom with a kid, and you're a young guy. Go back to school, go to Paris and get a girl your own age."

Well, he moved to Colorado, and I've seen him a few times since, and he never did get married. Obviously he never killed himself, either. He travels the world. I am awfully glad he didn't commit suicide. I don't happen to find suicide romantic. Romantic is roses, a diamond bracelet around a cock. Killing yourself is mental illness of the highest order. I'd prefer they live for me, not die for me—go on and live and stay strong and healthy and be grateful for what we had together.

Cradle robber I was not. These were not children; they were young men. Actually, perhaps emotionally a bit too young, and in need of too much attention, which is kind of childlike. I really wanted someone I didn't have to take care of; I wanted a man. But I wasn't prepared. A young guy just wants to have fun, and then they fall in love, don't you know? It's kind of silly and a bit boring. I was already a mother.

FIFTEEN
The Damage Done

Around the time of the "statutory rape" incident, at the end of 1980, Steven had his highly publicized motorcycle accident. A big deal was made of it at the time, but it was a poor excuse for an accident. It was actually a tiny, tiny dirtbike, one that is used to carry circus bears. It had a lawn mower motor. How fast could it go? It had a clutch and gears on it, but it's the kind of thing that a ten-year-old outgrows. It was a toy, and he was drunk, and he smashed into a tree with the housekeeper's daughter aboard. But he really went flying, and the heel of his foot was nearly torn off. It took about five hours of surgery to put his foot back together.

The physical damage he sustained as a result of that accident was real but, in the long run, insignificant compared to the damage being inflicted by his drug use. The manager of the band just said something to the *New York Times* about Steven discovering someone on the payroll who was called the promotion man, but was really buying drugs for the band. Stop the presses!

It was a very dark time, this period of heavy drug abuse. It was really scary. I think anyone involved with people in their drug-crazed darkness knows the feeling of having the devil around all the time. It was like living in hell, a drug hell, and anyone who does drugs knows that the sun doesn't shine. You become a vampire. Your mind and soul become Count Dracula's cellars.

There were moments when we'd get real high on heroin, and life seemed good. Heroin brought us to a level of normality, while cocaine spun Steven into psychosis. I'm not saying anything good about heroin here, believe me. It's just that once you're addicted, you don't ever really get high anymore, and you look for something with a kick. That's where cocaine differs from heroin. Steven says now that he can put his finger to his nose, and that triggers off a whole mechanism inside him that makes him want to get high. Just doing that sends him into the crazies. That's a serious fucking problem. There's something so deep and dark with this guy—I was there with it, and it was too much. What I felt of the darkness paled in comparison to what was going on inside him. And believe me, my life was black. So I don't know where the fuck he was.

Some of the stuff was unbelievable. We were once seeing a therapist together, and he took a little heart-shaped pillow and started stabbing and ripping it in front of the doctor. He was pointing to me and screaming, "You should have been a fucking nun," while he was ripping this pillow apart. I saw the doctor looking over at the door as though figuring out how fast an exit could be made, if necessary. Whoa!

Steven is a great lyricist, but the drugs made even the songwriting process very painful for him. The studio was paid by the hour, and the band would be waiting, plus every crew member. This became extremely expensive, particularly when he showed up two days late. He was always the last one there. He'd be off doing drugs while the other guys were trying to write the music, but they needed to have the words, so it was an endless cycle. He'd get there and lock himself in a room and do massive amounts of drugs in order to write some lyrics. He would end up going into the studio and writing on the hallway walls. I think "Dream On" and some other famous Aerosmith hits were composed on the walls outside of studios. He was so stoned and so desperate to be able to think of the words. This is the only way it worked.

In the early eighties there were horror stories all over the place: Steven lying on the street outside a drug hotel in the West 50's; Steven crapping in his pants and not knowing it. He was drugged out and hanging with this girl he met at his drug dealer's. He told me that he would buy her the economy size box of prophylactics so she could make the money turning tricks to buy his drugs. He was pissed off that I needed groceries and diapers. He hated me and beat me up all the time.

Even when I was pregnant he didn't care. He would punch me in the head and then turn around and be so kind. It was freaky. When I was about seven months pregnant I couldn't sleep on my stomach, so he took a huge knife and cut out a circle in the mattress so I could put my stomach in it. Though one could conceive of that as sweet, I thought it was a little scary. He was truly violent. He put pillows over my head and pinned me down. Then he'd talk, but I couldn't hear what he was saying. I only knew I had to stay very calm or I would lose air. When I did speak, I did so in a very low voice. If you raised your voice, there was too much static and it could set him off.

I was really afraid of him. But even so, I couldn't just leave. I was stuck in something. Where was there to go? What was I going to do? When women are battered, they always get asked, *Why didn't you just leave?* And we don't know the answer; we just can't. So I lied about the bruises. Tom Hamilton would get angry, Joe was freaked, and Johnny Thunders saw these huge rug burns on me and said, "What the fuck is that?" Nobody else said anything. So I would lie, even though Tom and Joe knew what was happening. I was embarrassed to tell the whole story, afraid he'd hurt me more. If I told, I thought it would get worse.

At the time, Steven was such a drug asshole, so dangerous to himself, not to mention to others, that he went out of his way to get himself arrested in Canada! It's true. This was after Keith Richards got arrested, and that must have really got him going.

Steven was going through the airport in Toronto, and he just took out a handful of hash and threw it on the floor. One of the roadies ran over and tried to pick it up, but he was too late, Steven had been seen, and he got busted. He threw it right on the floor in front of him, and with the reputation they already had, he knew the authorities were watching them carefully. So now he was a real rock star.

And then, of course, there were the guns. He had a huge gun collection. He'd wear a Walther PPK380, like James Bond, a semiautomatic loaded with hollow-point bullets. It goes in clean, but it blows your shoulder off on the way out; a high-powered piece of weaponry. One time I was downstairs in the New Hampshire house playing a Zeppelin album, getting his stuff ready to go on a trip, and there were other people who worked for us in the kitchen, and I didn't hear Steven calling my name, and all of a sudden, *Boom!* He shot out the stereo. He said, "Can you hear me now?" I said, "You fucking bastard, that's really cool, you're leaving and I have no music!"

Another time he went upstairs, and he was really angry. Suddenly I heard the gun go off. I was so afraid, I thought he'd shot himself. I didn't want to go upstairs. I called his name over and over, and when he didn't answer, I knew I'd have to go up the stairs and look. When I did, I found him standing there with a smirk on his face.

Even the drug dealers hated Steven. One famous dealer asked David Krebs if Steven was worth more to him dead or alive. It was ironic, actually, because when you think of it, when you're doing drugs, being dead or alive is accidental. Sometimes it's nothing more than luck. One girl does a hit and she's gone. The next one, who scored from a different guy down the street, lived. If you've ever had too many drugs in your body, you know "this could be it." It overwhelms you, and all you can say is, "See ya." There's nothing else.

I don't know why I survived. I certainly came close to death at least once. I overdosed with Steven and had to be resuscitated. I saw the white light and all this kind of stuff after shooting up a massive cocaine hit in New Hampshire. It was really spooky. Steven was scared to death. I had a grand mal seizure, something even he had never seen, though I certainly had seen him go through many of them. Ugh, shooting up. It is such a dirty, ugly, unfeminine thing.

No one should abuse anything, and I must say, *Don't try it, don't do it, you're not missing anything.* I'm not doing it anymore and I don't miss it. Shooting up is so disgusting, it is the bottom of the pit. It's like you have nothing left in you, and you still want to see how far down you can take yourself. There is nothing worse than needles. When you hit that, you've gone into the devil's workshop. You're gone. You're over.

Do I sound like Nancy Reagan? Good, so be it. Drugs start off innocently enough. You're being naughty, *ha ha ha.* We're so wild, and then within no time you are suddenly so committed to this stuff.

It quickly becomes more than an albatross around your neck or a monkey on your back, it's a goddamn gorilla, a monster that's part of your life, that *is* your life. Once you start, you've given up. The weekend warrior is strung out, and all the beautiful things you could have had are gone into your veins or up your nose, and life is shit.

Every good thing that Steven and I could have had together was tainted by the drugs. There is no good time when there are drugs. You don't feel good; they make you stupid and irrational. They put you in another world, so how can you say you're having a good time? Leaving this space, this body, this dimension for some fucked-up delusion? This dimension is very cool, and you can do a lot with it. Once you take drugs, you're nowhere. You're not here. You're not there.

That's how I was on them, especially cocaine. I hate cocaine more than anything in this world. You say, "I love you," or, "This is cool," and it's not you talking or feeling that, it's the drug. Cocaine really made Steven psychotic, too. And there's always anger. Anybody who has done drugs can tell you, it wasn't that good. We were sick more than we were high, and unhappy much more than we were feeling good.

A lot of people think I'm smarter because of what I've been through. Drugs didn't make me smarter. They made me aware of things I shouldn't have ever had to deal with. Why should I know what a jail cell looks like? Why should I have to know what the barrel of a gun looks like in my face? Why should I know fists in my face? Why should I know someone's hatred because I kept them from taking drugs?

I'll never be as healthy as I was because of the drugs. There is damage. My immune system will never be the same. If you're a woman, you're much more delicate inside, and your reproductive organs go to hell. How can you pour poison on a rosebush and expect to grow a beautiful rose? I catch every cold, I catch every bug, and I have to take more vitamin C than anyone I've known in my entire life.

And I have a warped sense of reality when it comes to people. I don't trust people. I haven't been with a man for years because of one horrible, disgusting, drugged-out trip. The issue that continues to haunt me is that Steven and I could have been something beautiful. A beautiful child, a house, a husband, a wife, it should have been something beautiful that grew spiritually. But my life with Steven was being destroyed every single day. It was being ripped away by drugs, and there's nothing I can say that's good about it. It's the only thing in my life that I regret. It was an ugly, dirty world. It's the epitome of a walk on the dark side.

So much innocence was taken from me during that time. Part of my womanness was taken away. I told Steven that once, and he said, "What is it you want?" and I said "I just want to be a woman." And he looked at me like he really understood.

Although Steven Tyler and I were legally married for nine years, I don't want you to think I lived in this drug hell for that long. I'd be dead now. At the time we were married, in September of 1978, we were on the road most of the time. In 1979 Aerosmith started to fall apart; first Joe Perry left, and then Brad Whitford. Both were replaced, but there were lots of problems with the new members. Albums weren't selling, and the touring was getting erratic because of Steven's drug use.

In 1981 Steven and I sublet the apartment in New York from the actor Tony LoBianco so Steven could work on an album and be closer to the big drug dealers. I took a trip to St. Barth, St. Martin, and Florida with the baby to get away from everything, and to get off heroin, and when I was gone, Steven and some girlfriend and a drug dealer who was living with them trashed the apartment and were thrown out. He broke all the mirrors and smashed everything breakable. I guess it was a cocaine fit, because that's what coke did to him.

All of my stuff was supposedly packed up and moved to a warehouse in Boston, where there was this mysterious "flood," and everything I owned was thrown out. Things that had been in my family for hundreds of years, carriage covers that had a bead for each newborn—gone. Steven said they got mildewed and couldn't be saved. I replied that he could have let me go through my own things and use some baking soda on the mildew; that should have been my decision. But he had decided to just throw my things out. The few things that were left in New York had been ripped, because I was so small (from all the

coke, let's face it), and somebody bigger than me had
been trying on my custom-made leather stuff and tear-
ing it.

Steven had wanted me to come back to New York
then, but instead I insisted that he come to Florida so
that I could see what condition he was in before I
returned into his life. When he came down, he was
cooking up coke constantly and freebasing away like
mad. It was a horrible, horrible time. I decided I never
wanted to be with him again. He was just too far
gone.

I wanted to be in New York, apart from him, and
just with my daughter. I'd slipped so far down, I
didn't want any of my friends in New York to see
me. I wanted to work this out for myself, get rid of
the drugs and give my daughter some of the attention
she needed.

That was really the end of Steven and me living
together as husband and wife. We would see each
other and even had sex a few times in the next few
years, plus there was the horrendous trip to Hawaii,
but in effect we were separated. So Steven moved into
the Mayflower Hotel on Central Park West, and I
went to live in the apartment of Jack Douglas in the
West 70's between Central Park West and Columbus
Avenue. This was 1982, and it was the apartment Jack
had been living in when he was producing John Lennon's last album. In December the reporters came
looking for Jack to talk about John's death in 1980.
I was doing drugs again.

I couldn't maintain this apartment, I couldn't get it

together. Steven would come and visit and have the nerve to complain that because there were no plants, that I wasn't making the place presentable enough. Mind you, he wasn't even living there. I asked for money to buy plants, when I was really trying to get money to buy diapers and things for Mia. This was a little kid, there was no money, and he was not there for us. He arrived unannounced any time he wanted. Actually, days, weeks, months meant nothing to me. Each day was survival.

I would have to go over to his managers' office and cry, "I need some money!" and they didn't want to know, they just didn't care. One time Jack Douglas went with me to the accountant's office. He growled at the accountant, "You better give this girl money for her baby's diapers," and he did. Jack was seriously going to kick some butt.

I have to say, though, that my apartment was kind of creepy. It was the basement floor and subbasement of a brownstone, very dark. I had a girl staying with me for a while helping me out—a really nice girl. She needed a place to stay, and I couldn't pay her, but she helped me with the baby.

I'll never forget one thing that happened there. Steven came to visit, and he was in total drug dementia. He'd been shooting massive amounts of heroin. He had invested ten thousand dollars in a heroin deal, and the check for the dope had come from his office. On this day, he was standing facing forward, and I was standing next to him and talking, blah blah blah, and he wasn't looking in my direction. Then his head turned really slowly toward me, and when I looked in his eyes, he didn't look like Steven anymore. I thought I saw the eyes of a demon, the thing that was living inside him.

It was like I had made contact with another entity. I got the shivers. It was more terrifying than anything I've ever seen in a movie. I swear, if his eyes had started glowing red, that would have been it. My hair would have turned white, and I'd be babbling and drooling, or I would have died of fright right there. Everything around me had become dark and dirty and evil. I ran into the bedroom and wrote a note, pinned it on the door, and shut myself in there. It said, "Please don't knock. Just don't be here when I come out."

He left after being there for some time. He'd been in the bathroom. I opened the door, and there was a spoon in the light fixture, and the syringe was on top of the medicine cabinet. At that point I started saying to myself, "You've got to go," and I started becoming strong enough physically, consciously, and emotionally to say, "Go! This has got to end." I was clearing out and cleaning up.

I called a girlfriend, packed a bag, rented a car, and drove to New Hampshire. I went to see David Krebs to say goodbye; we did two lines of coke each, and I was behind the wheel within two hours. And that was it. That was my own personal bottom. I would stay in New Hampshire for nine years, and it was a hard time, but I know I saved my life by getting my

battered little ass out of New York that day in 1982.
We got back to New Hampshire in time for Mia's
fourth birthday.

I knew I had to do this for this child. I had to go.
I looked in the mirror, and I looked like death. And
I probably would have died. God said, "You're going
to die." So I took my little girl to the country, and I
stayed there.

Steven visited us periodically in New Hampshire.
I always knew when he was going to show up. He
would drive up himself. I was living in the Big House
then. Mia would go, "Daddy's here!" I'd be a little
afraid and a little happy at the same time. I never
knew if he was going to spend the night; he could
always stay at a hotel or drive back. It was only three
hours to Boston, where he had an apartment that I
never saw.

If he said he was spending the night, it was taken
for granted by him, then, that we would have sex. It
wasn't taken for granted by me. He'd say, "I'm staying over. I'm spending the night." I'd tell him, "Oh,
great. You have to sleep in pajamas then," and he'd
say, "No, I never sleep in clothes." And then I'd sleep
in pajamas. I wouldn't get ready for sex. He had abandoned us, and I was very hurt and afraid. I didn't want
to have sex with this guy, but he was still my husband, and I always thought that we'd work it out
somehow, but he was fucking me over so badly. He
was living with some bitch, and he'd be behaving as
if nothing had ever gone wrong.

I'd say it was only about three or four times that we had sex out of the ten times he came to visit me, between the time I left New York for New Hampshire in 1982 and our divorce in 1987. After the divorce, he was leaving and I was standing at the washing machine, and he must have liked the way I looked, and he came up behind me and put his hands on my hips and said, "If I had more time." I said, "Get off me."

Each time we did it, it was like he got what he wanted. And afterward he'd say, "I know you can never forgive me," and I'd say, "I can forgive you, but I can never forget." He would say he'd always love me, and that after me he'd never marry again. Of course, six months later he remarried.

When he walks into a place, he acts as if he owns it. He acts that way at the apartment where Mia and I are now living. We'd be sitting watching TV on those nights that he'd stay over, and he'd want to go to bed. He'd say, "Let's turn the TV off and let's go to bed." And I would say, "What do you mean, *let's* go to bed?" and he'd say, "Well, I want to go to sleep now," and I'd say, "Well, why don't you sleep here on the sofa?" and he'd say, "I don't think so." He'd get indignant about everything.

He kept his clothes up at New Hampshire until long after the divorce. I didn't want him to sleep naked next to me. Then he'd crawl up next to me, and it would just happen. There was no heavy making out, but we would have sex, and I would hope deep down that it was going to change from then on, that he would want to do the right thing. But for him, sleeping with a woman is nothing. The next morning I would cry, not so much for me, but for Mia. She didn't want her daddy to leave. She'd cry and hide and hang on to his leg, and I'd get so angry I'd have to pick her up and take her to another part of the house until he was gone.

I never gave up hope until the paperwork for the divorce started. The last time we ever had sex was about six or seven months before the divorce became final. The feelings were there, but they were all frayed, all these little threads hanging down. I was still in love with him, I had this child, this responsibility, and I had no one to talk to. He would always call me on the phone and play with my emotions.

Now Steven is all recovered and the band is all "sober," and they make a big deal of being Champions of Rehab, and a Model for Youth, and Rock Without Drugs. Let me tell you a story: In early 1990 sober Steven was coming to visit Mia at school in New York and to speak to the kids. I warned the people who ran the school that this was not a good idea. This was the Professional Children's School, and he was coming during Park Day, a day in Central Park. And I had the feeling that he'd use the opportunity to reminisce about how he used to drop LSD and trip in the park and cut school, and what a cool youth he was. It's all a wink and a nod when it comes to drugs, now that he's Mr. Recovery Poster Boy. It's as if to say, it isn't so bad, really, because look at me now.

And these kids at the school idolized him so much because he's this big rock star and the father of one of them, and sure enough, he tells them about the LSD in the park and how he never went to school. They're just lapping it up, these students. Not that I know what to tell kids, but I think I know what not to tell them if you're a rock hero. I'm not a drug counselor, but I know that what he did was irresponsible. It really was loathsome.

SIXTEEN
Cleaning Up My Act

I started getting straight, or making the effort and suffering through a bunch of setbacks, in 1982. Getting straight doesn't mean getting perfect, it means getting rid of your drug addiction. There are still a lot more problems to face afterward, but without the drugs, at least you're ready to battle them with a relatively clear mind.

It was when we were living on West End Avenue that I decided to get off heroin. I went to a public methadone clinic and a private doctor gave me a large amount of methadone, enough to fill a giant empty Scope bottle, and I took Mia and went to St. Martin and then to Florida. I took little nips from the bottle whenever I started to get achy. I was on the highest dose of methadone they give, 97 milligrams. I took just enough to get rid of the pain in the back of my neck, which was where I would always start to feel the need for dope. So I'd take that nip, just to make it go away. I was determined not to substitute a methadone addiction for a heroin addiction, so I weaned myself from the methadone as well. I finished the mouthwash bottle after about two weeks, and I started to come back from the dead. I went walking with Mia, and I was feeling better. I don't recommend this method to everyone. I had put myself in charge of my own therapy, and that can be very dangerous.

When I left New York for New Hampshire in 1982, I left my heroin habit behind. I started drinking more, but there was no heroin and no pills. I started getting some of my memory back, and I got a little bit of help from the natural food stores. B-complex vitamins are great for a person who's been on drugs. B-complex restored my mind and took away the depression.

There would be little slips. Steven's cronies were always coming around, and naturally they had drugs with them. Some old dealer would come by with an ounce and break it out and tempt me. So I'd do drugs all over again, but this time I would say to myself—and really believe it—"This sucks, I hate this, I've always hated this. Why am I doing this? I don't have to. I want to get away from this."

I started saying no to Steven's friends, the dealers. I'd just clench my fist and turn down their offerings. I thought, *If I continue to do drugs, I will be letting down my daughter.* And they really tempt you, these dealers, they do not like taking no for an answer. They get really upset when you don't bite. It turned me on to see them getting pissed off, and that helped me say no. At first you play these little games with them, because you're used to saying, "Sure, man, whatever! Only don't shoot up because my kid's in the house." That was something I always hated, because I was afraid someone would die, and then what would I say to the police? I remembered that picture of Lenny Bruce lying on the floor of his bathroom, dead of an OD, and I thought about his daughter, Kitty, and what a horrifying thing that must be for a child to see.

It all goes back to that hopeless dream I had that when I brought a child into this world, my husband would straighten up and we would be happy. He asked for the child, he asked me to marry him, I'm going to give him what he wants, I'm going to make him so happy. But the disease goes so deep, and there I was, in danger of being a UPI photo: ROCK WIFE DEAD!

Well, I was back in New Hampshire. Shortly afterward, Steven and I made that awful attempt to patch things up, this time in Hawaii. As soon as we got there, the drug dealers were waiting for Steven at the airport. I had left Mia with Steven's sister and her cousin, Julia. When we returned to the mainland, I went on the road with him for about a week. We had separate hotel rooms every night. He was a mess. He was on the phone crying all the time to Teresa, I guess. He needed drugs. I went back to New Hampshire.

He sent bouquets of roses every once in a while, with notes that said, "Think about London, think London, love!" He'd be in an airplane and phone from the plane: "I'm flying right over you now," but I knew he was a few hundred miles away and didn't know the difference.

Then, in 1984, Joe Perry and Brad Whitford came to see Steven at the Orpheus Theater in Boston, and they decided to re-form the original Aerosmith. They had a new manager, Tim Collins. Tim tried to enlist my support in this Aerosmith renaissance. He had Joe call me, knowing I would never hang up on Joe Perry. They promised me "she" (Teresa) would be gone, and everything would be peachy once again.

And I believed it, because I really wanted to. I blamed everything on drugs. They promised me that Steven would get clean. I thought we'd have a cozy year of therapy, and then we would be a family again. *This Tim Collins seems like a really nice guy*, I thought. Boy, was it ever a load of shit.

By late 1985 I knew the reunion wasn't going to happen. I got letters from the managers telling me I had better plan carefully for my future, whatever that meant. I think Joe and Elissa lost their house; things were getting really bad. Tim was telling me that Steven was so far gone that he'd give him talcum powder and he would snort it up and think he was getting high. And there was a violent scene in Tim's office when Steven wanted money to go to the Cape, and they knew it was for drugs. Steven smashed an antique box that had belonged to Tim's mother, and Tim said, "Look, Mister, this is it," and that, as I understand it, was the turning point.

It was a wild time. They were calling Steven's girl-friend Snaggletooth behind Steven's back and saying she could open beer cans with her teeth. When Steven came to see Mia, he asked her, "What would you like Daddy to do?" and she said, "Come home." But he told me he couldn't leave Teresa after all she'd done for him. I said, "Get out, then." He still wanted me to give him blowjobs, he still wanted to sleep with me, and I gave in, about four or five times over the two-year period from 1985 to 1986. I got pregnant one of those times and had an abortion. Steven will find out about that if he ever reads this book.

That was the second time I had aborted Steven's child. The first time was when we were living on West End Avenue in 1981. I got $250 from David Krebs, and I was in Women's Hospital, and Steven called, and guilt flooded through my body. He said, "Are you having an abortion? Because if you are, I don't want you to do it." And I said, "Oh, no, it's just a checkup!" He bought it, and I limped out of there like a sack of shit. I immediately went and got high on methadone.

So I spent 1982–1991 in New Hampshire, the last half of that time as a divorced single parent. It was a nightmare. My body was physically wiped out. I didn't want to do any drugs, and the only people who came around were people who wanted to get high. This was not the life I wanted for my little girl, so I had a nervous breakdown. Not a mental breakdown in which you have delusions, but one in which your body collapses and you have no strength, mentally, emotionally, physically. My nervous system was shot from doing drugs, stress, and giving up drugs. There were times when I thought my skin would catch on fire, that's how lousy I felt.

My divorce became final on November 13, 1987. I got screwed. It's really complicated, but mainly my lawyers don't want me to say much about it because it's being contested right now. Suffice it to say, I lost everything. The judge thought I was a greedy old witch. They ripped me apart. The original agreement was for Steven to give me $450 a month and $300 in child support; we had a thousand-gallon oil tank, and all that money was going toward heating the house. My oil bill was a thousand dollars! You figure out what's left to live on.

I got shafted. I had asked David Krebs, Steven's former manager, to help me find a divorce lawyer, and he got me a college pal of his, Peter Shukat. I asked about royalties for Mia, because the songwriting royalties could make Mia secure for her life, and I recall David saying, "You'll never get those. Forget about it."

Well, I thought that David had nothing to do with the band or its earning potential at that point, and that's why I asked him to help me with the divorce. Guess what? David just sold the publishing rights to Sony for $24 million. To me that means he controlled it, and he did indeed have a great deal to do with the band and its earning potential. And the publishing royalties would keep coming for seventy-five years, so that a song written in 1985 would bring in money until the year 2060. If he had arranged for Mia to have any publishing royalties, there would be less for him to sell! I'm oversimplifying, but in my mind that's what David's help was all about.

If I could sell the house in New Hampshire, I could get the money. The house was falling apart and needed more in structural repairs than I could afford. I cleaned it as best I could. It didn't sell. The agreement gave me two years to sell the house, after which it reverted back to Steven. If I could sell it, I could keep a certain amount of the money. I painted the house myself. I got on my hands and knees and scrubbed the inside of the house. I borrowed some guy's truck because I had no car, and I tried to make these cosmetic changes so that the house would be marketable. The property itself was not chopped liver. It was lakefront property, worth about one thousand dollars a square foot, with one big, very badly built house, a smaller house, and the foundation for a garage. It was beautiful there in the summer, and if you ski, I guess it was good during the winter, too.

I thought I could clean it up, sell it, and get the hell out. The roof in the main house was leaking, water was coming in through the light fixtures, the pipes weren't insulated and were always freezing, and when the lake iced over the floors of the house buckled like waves on the ocean. The wiring wasn't traceable, it was just stuck in there. It must have needed at least a hundred thousand dollars' worth of work.

My nest was not built very well. As it was, who would buy it?

Earlier that year a notice was tacked to the house saying that it was going to be auctioned off by the bank because Steven hadn't been paying the mortgage. I had to swear under oath that Steven and I weren't filing for divorce just to get out of paying the mortgage! I had to put another sign on the house: THERE IS NO AUCTION HERE. What a sorry sight I was! Practically my only friends in the area were some bikers I had met through Steven. I never had known people like that before, yet they were very nice and helped me tremendously. They knew about plumbing, and they would go underground and work on the pipes, which were a disaster. They were doing work that I couldn't afford to have done. During the divorce proceedings Steven tried to paint me as this biker tramp, but I never touched any of them, so it was all a lie.

My days during those years were torture, because I had this weariness that wouldn't go away. I would get up and give Mia a bath, then make her cinnamon toast, stay up with her until around 10 A.M., and try to get her to take a nap. Then I'd lie down and rest. This was when she was between three and four years old. By the time she got to preschool, I was "resting" nearly all the time.

Then the eating started. I became a compulsive eater, and I could think of nothing but food all day and all night. I'd start cooking, and I'd make these huge meals from food I'd charge at the grocery store.

I missed the New York restaurants, where you could go and get any kind of meal any time you wanted it. There was no place to eat up in New Hampshire, and there was no one to help me cook. I went wild for bread. Cheese bread, poppy-seed bread, you name it, I made it, bread, bread, bread. Then I started on meats. I hated meat, and suddenly I'm cooking rack of lamb and loving it. I gained sixty-five pounds in about three months.

I wasn't a purger, though. I'd eat and then sit quietly and rest until I knew I wouldn't throw up. Somehow I felt warm and safe. Then I'd think about eating again. I'd be up in the middle of the night cooking eggs and bacon and making sandwiches.

If I found someone to eat with, that would be fabulous because then I could make even more food, but then I'd try not to eat quite as much as I ordinarily would have eaten if I were alone. I would try and be ladylike about it. The people in town thought I was pregnant because I had gained weight so quickly. I had to eat. It was comforting. I had no comfort of any kind, really. Mia needed love and she wanted to love me, but I didn't know how to love her. I didn't know what I was doing.

I was smoking cigarettes as well, and learning how to drink. Joe Perry always told me I should learn how to drink, and Steven's mother told me that, too. I discovered whiskey. Seagram's Seven Crown, of all things. I think it was big with male drunks in the 1940s. People retch even thinking of it, but I got to the point where I could drink it straight. It tastes sort of like caramel.

It was a sickening way to live. I didn't want drugs, and food was legal, food was easy to get, and who was going to say anything? I wasn't being bad. Eating is a good thing to do, eating is all right. I got so fat I couldn't even cross my legs, and I had to wear my old maternity clothes. On his visits, Steven would make jokes about buying me some muumuus next time he went to Hawaii, or he'd say he wanted to knock me down, but there weren't enough people around to get me back up. A friend told me that the next time he said something about my weight, I should say to him, "I may be overweight, but you're ugly, and I can lose the weight." I did say it, and he looked at me in amazement. For the first time, I was answering back instead of crying or cowering in another room.

Then something clicked. I had a mirrored shower, and one day I just looked at myself and started sobbing. I thought, *Oh my God, what have I done?* And I wondered if it was too late. I didn't know how to stop anything, but I started putting notes on the refrigerator: "Why are you here?" I put the cigarettes far away so I would have to go all the way downstairs to get one, and I put the whiskey in another place that was difficult to reach. I was a total slob. I had become a fat floozy, a heifer, cows mooed at me, I never wore black and white together.

What a great adventure I had had! From a skeleton walking the streets of New York, afraid to be seen by my old friends, to an obese shut-in living in a New Hampshire hovel. The former toast of downtown New York, Andy Warhol's glamorous prop and confidante, the queen of the rock-and-roll road. Things were going backward and inside out. I was clean of drugs, but I was a gross, housebound whiskey mama. No! Stop! Help! I have a child. I owe her more than this, I owe myself more, I owe God more.

God saved me. He got me and my daughter back to New York, a brand-new Cyrinda, mother, socialite, and fabulous persona redux.

SEVENTEEN

Outta' There, Back Here

I was badly advised on my divorce settlement. I was told that the band was destitute and that there probably would never be any more money than there was now, and that I was better off taking whatever I could get.

Aerosmith had come back together and had released *Done with Mirrors* for Geffen Record Company in January of 1986. It climbed into the thirties on the charts, but I was sure one album wouldn't make the band rich all over again. It takes selling a lot of records to recoup the advance that a record company gives you when you sign with them, and then it takes a long time for the accountants to get to work and pay you what's owed to you, if anything. That happens in even the best of record companies, which Geffen is, of course. In any case, things were starting to cook once more for the reborn Aerosmith at the time of our divorce, but money wasn't rolling in.

That shouldn't have mattered, though. During our

divorce proceedings in fall 1987, the *Permanent Vacation* album reached number eleven, and the single "Dude Looks Like a Lady" was in the Top Twenty. The *Permanent Vacation* tour was selling out all over the world, and if the cash wasn't at hand, it was sure in the pipeline. When the lawyers told me, "You better take this. Who knows if he'll ever do better?" they were wrong, plain and simple. Steven was already doing better, much better, financially.

In all fairness, Steven Tyler's wife and daughter were entitled to more than a house with no foundation and doors and windows through which the snow blew. But I signed the papers, and all of a sudden I was divorced. I had two years to sell the shitty house or it would revert back to Steven.

I reopened our divorce case in 1988. Aerosmith's song "Angel" got to number three in April of that year, and the group was really on a roll. That shows you how out of touch I was. It was at this point that their comeback was acknowledged to be as remarkable as any ever seen in the rock era. And all I had was a house I couldn't sell because there was no money for repairs. I called David Krebs for help and advice, but he said there was nothing he could do.

The 1988 legal wrangling got me nowhere. I might as well have been slamming my head against the wall. Steven's business managers and lawyers were very good, the best that money could buy, and they took advantage of me. I was stuck in New Hampshire, and it was fucking bleak. I had to trade parts of Steven's

boat for a cord of wood because Mia and I were freezing, and Steven came up and wanted to know what
the hell happened to his boat. "I burned it so your
daughter wouldn't freeze to death, you bastard," I
snapped.

A kid who worked for David Krebs came by the
house to check things out, to see what else I had
traded in for firewood, and he was shocked by what
he saw. I was in rags. My phone and electricity had
been turned off. "I didn't know how bad it was," he
confessed to me. "I always knew Steven was a little
strange, but I can't believe he'd let his family live
like this." And the kid went back and told Steven that
he hated him and would never speak to him again.

Finally, after going through the divorce and the fu-
tile replay of it, and all the shit I'd been through with
my health and the compulsive eating and the drugs
and now the drinking, my mind started to clear, and
I wanted outta' there. I wanted to be back in New
York. Fuck New Hampshire, cold, dreary, moronic,
nowhere New Hampshire. Why should I stay there a
minute longer? This was Steven's domain, where he
spent his summers, where his parents had their "resort." Why was I here? I was in my thirties, and my
energy was returning, and most importantly, Mia was
growing up and I didn't want her partaking of the
noncivilization that surrounded us. Why shouldn't she
have the benefits of New York City culture and a
good school? If you were a girl in New Hampshire,
by the time you were in the eighth grade you were

either a scholar and getting the hell out of there or you were pregnant and a drunk.

Cheryl Krebs, David's estranged wife, came up to visit me and she saw how dreadful my condition was, although she was tactful enough not to come right out and say it. As if I needed to be told. Before she left, she invited me to come and visit her in New York. I left Mia with her aunt and cousin, got a really cheap plane ticket, and went to New York. It is forty-five minutes away by plane, but in my mind it was like going to a whole other planet.

There have been so many different Cyrindas since the one who first got off that plane in New York from Oklahoma back in 1971. I'll bet you think there was something glamorous about each one of them: the bride of two rock stars, the cocaine skeleton, the walking companion of Greta Garbo, the prey of Ike Turner, the toast of Max's Kansas City, the fags' fave rave. But there was nothing glamorous about this fat hausfrau standing in Cheryl's kitchen, looking out of the window at the buildings and sobbing. I was back in New York. I'd been gone nine years. I wanted to live there again. I didn't want to go back to New Hampshire.

"Please don't make me go back there," I begged Cheryl, as though it were something under her control. She said I could stay with her. But of course my daughter was still up in Palookaville, and I had this property, and there was unfinished business back there which I knew I had to handle. I had finally reached the point where I realized I couldn't evade my responsibilities.

During my visit to New York, this giddiness overtook me. Some guiding spirit took hold of the part of me that takes care of myself and my daughter, and I called the archdiocese of New York and asked about parochial schools for children. I called two of them that sounded good and made appointments to visit them. My feet hurt, because it had been so long since I'd walked on pavement, and I was so overweight.

What did I think I was going to do? The schools that I was checking out cost thousands of dollars a year. Still, I went ahead. I felt very safe, as if I were in a bubble, as if I were the mother of a daughter whose daddy was rich, and I was searching for the very best place for her to be. After all, Mia did have a rich father, and it said in the divorce agreement that he had to pay for parochial school—at least I got that. They weren't paying my electric bills, because that wasn't in the settlement, but the Catholic school thing was in the settlement and I intended to push it.

I got a simple black dress and visited these schools. I felt so comfortable. A kind of ease came over me. I had suffered and come out on the other side, and I knew a better life was going to happen for me and for my daughter. The woman at Marymount said, "We'd like to see the child. We'd like to see her Friday."

I had no more money. How was I going to get to New Hampshire, get Mia, and bring her back? But I wasn't panicked; I was walking around in this weird

cloud, it felt very safe and warm, like a guardian angel was helping me through all of this.

I called a travel agent right away and she said,
"Wait, I'll see what comes up on the computer." Then
she said, "I can't believe it, there's a special deal. I
can get a round trip for the two of you for ninety-
nine dollars."

"I'll take it, I'll take it!" I blurted. I totally believe
God wanted me to come back to New York.

I flew to New Hampshire from Newark and I said
to Mia, "You're going to New York, you're going to
be interviewed." And she was like, "What for? I don't
want to go there." She didn't know New York, she
hadn't been there since she was three, and she was
eleven then. I explained, "You're going to take some
tests for a school in New York." I was crying, and
she asked, "Why do you always cry when you talk
about New York?" and I said, "Honey, you don't understand. My heart beats when I'm in New York. My
blood flows when I'm there."

I was delirious with excitement when the two of us
got to town. We had to take a bus from the airport to
the Port Authority Terminal, and I was warning Mia
to hang on to my jacket, don't let go, I have to hold
the bags, you have to hold me, there are runaways
and drug addicts and scary people. She was hanging
on for dear life, and I was giddy; I thought I was
going to bust.

We stayed at Cheryl's house. Mia passed the tests,
and the school wanted a $1500 deposit. I asked
Steven's people for it, and they sent it without asking

any questions (at first). It all seemed to be part of God's master plan. When Steven heard that his people had paid the deposit, he freaked, and he wouldn't let us have the money it would take to move to New York. He wouldn't pay to fix the house, but he didn't want me moving to New York, either. Steven said, "It's just a geographical difference. You are who you are." I recognized this as AA bullshit brainwashing. Well, that's wonderful wisdom, I felt like telling Steven, but I'm not from New Hampshire, you are. I'm from New York, I have custody of our child, and I want to raise her in New York. Why did you pay for the school if you're not going to pay for us to live near the school? I was breaking out in hives and chain-smoking cigarettes. I couldn't believe this.

I got a good lawyer and initiated legal action against Steven. I went before a judge. Steven wasn't there. He sent his lawyer, who said, "Your honor, we think we should wait." My lawyer said, "Your honor, she interviewed and tested, was accepted, and the school was paid the deposit. They can't pull out now. The child has been accepted at Marymount, one of the best schools in New York."

I saw that this judge was not looking at anybody. The judge said, "I don't know where your client is. Why didn't he show up? He paid. Why would you not want the child to go to this school when you've paid the deposit? I'll be back, and Mrs. Tyler will have the order in fifteen minutes."

Fabulous. Steven's lawyer was screaming, "My client this, my client that," and he was completely flustered. The judge said, "Shut up, brother," and he left the room.

We got the order. It said that even though the defendant was not in court, paying the funds will not cause him any distress and therefore this child will be in the school of her mother's choice.

Then the judge wanted to know where the child was going to live. He said that since the child was going to be in a school in a safe neighborhood, she must live in a safe neighborhood. The lawyer said that Queens had lots of perfectly safe neighborhoods, and she could take the subway to the school. The judge said something like, "No way. I don't care if you have to pay to have her live at the Plaza Hotel, the child will live in a safe, nice neighborhood, near the school."

Mia and I ended up in a tiny apartment on Madison Avenue. We were supposed to live there for three months, but we stayed there five years. It was so small that we kept bumping into each other. Mia couldn't have friends over and had no privacy, and neither did I. We painted it red and painted her room purple, anything to pretend it wasn't a shoe box. Once I squeezed twenty people in there, and no one could move. Finally, I couldn't live like that anymore, and my lawyers and Steven's lawyers once again went into battle. Early in 1996 we moved into the apartment we live in now, on East 68th Street. Mia has her own bathroom, and it's just divine, and I love it.

I devoted my first year in New York to getting Mia settled into her new home and her new school and new life. I saw none of my old friends, and until I lost weight I wasn't eager to see them. Andy Warhol had died on my birthday in 1987, and that blew my mind because how can you find anybody without Andy around? But little by little I started running into people. I saw Liz Derringer when we were having lunch at Mortimer's; Sam Green was there, too, and I sent a note over to him. He jumped up and ran over and said, "Oh my God, Cyrinda, you're back and, er, there's so much more of you!" I thought, *Oh good, I'm home, someone is telling me the truth.* Yeah, I'm here, I'm fat, I'm in New York. Deal with it, because food was still my drug of choice.

I saw Jed Johnson, who directed me in *Bad* (and who died in the crash of TWA flight 800 in July 1996; it went down practically right across from his beautiful beach house on Fire Island), and Sylvia Miles and Paul Morrissey and Geraldine Smith and Cherry Vanilla and, of course, Leee Childers. It's so hard to make a list of those of us who call ourselves the survivors; by the time you finish it someone is already off the list.

The ones who are still here might have found what they've wanted out of life. The ones who aren't here, maybe they were pretending, playacting, and they went too far looking for something that was never there. Oh, how the hell do I know? I miss them by the hundreds: When someone we loved died about five years ago, Penny Arcade said, "You know, I think there are now more of them than there are of us."

I'd love to believe I'll get to heaven and there will

be Candy, Dorothy Dean, Lillian Roxon, Mickey Ruskin, Peter Allen, Jackie and Johnny and Tinkerbelle, and it would be like the Back Room all over again— with the same jukebox, I hope.

The people you love, the people you have loved, are so precious. Friends who are in their thirties, forties, and fifties say that they lose people as fast as, or faster than, their parents do. You had to be tough to have been a butterfly in New York or in rock and roll in the sixties and seventies, and still be here. I always look at Iggy Pop; he's the saint of survivors. I love him like a brother. He may be the smartest of us all, and he is probably the toughest. As long as Iggy's on our team, we're okay. Is Steven Tyler on our team? As a husband, a human being, a father? That's a good question.

I see and talk to Steven with some frequency because of our daughter. One of the things we always shared was our opinions of each other's appearance, but now when I see him I really don't want to talk about the way he looks, because I can tell he's trying to hold on to his youth with every ounce of strength he's got left in him. Six years ago he made me hold my hand out, and he pinched the skin on top of my hand and let go, and it went right back in place. I asked, "What are you doing?" He said, "Oh, I just want to see what your skin does, how springy it is," and he did it to himself, and his skin just kind of stayed up there and then went down. He exclaimed, "Well! Overweight people have firmer skin. They don't get lines. You're lucky you're overweight because it makes your skin look better." Would you say this is denial from a forty-eight-year-old person?

If we're talking about a certain activity or whatever, he'll say something like, "Oh, leave that to the young people, we've had our turn. We did that, we had our fun." Well, maybe he had his fun. He sure stole mine. I'm a little bitter about that. But he'd say to me, "Oh, you and I are so alike. We just don't look old, our skin looks so great! You don't have any wrinkles or lines." And I would be thinking, *Steven, put your glasses on. Look at me, and more importantly, look at yourself.*

Steven can't stay away from the mirror. David Bowie didn't look in the mirror all the time. David Johansen didn't look in the mirror all the time. They'd just look and fluff and walk. Steven sits there and it's really a serious thing for him. He doesn't move. He's hypnotized. He'd get upset whenever he gained weight. "Do I look like I'm getting fat? I think I'm gaining weight! We have to change what we're eating. I have to look skinny and young. The kids want me to look youthful."

He's never said anything to me about any surgical procedures, but when he was raving about what beautiful skin we both had, I felt like saying to him, "Steven, I think a face-lift would do you wonders." But I don't say anything like that because I don't care. When he was doing all those drugs and he made one of his several attempts to stop or cut back, he'd gain weight and actually begin to look a little healthy, and that would freak him out and he'd go right back to

drugs. He wanted to get his act together, he wanted
to get healthy, but he didn't have the power to do it.
He'd fly off the handle if I brought it up.

Steven is so wonderfully talented, though. I always
wondered how he could write songs that were so sensitive and romantic and intuitive, and then turn around
and be such a clod. The songs seem to have nothing
to do with his life. I wonder where they come from.
You'd expect such songs to come from a young, sensitive American artist. Then again, Jim Morrison was
a young, sensitive American artist, and look what
kind of human being he was. I would compare Steven
to Morrison, and he thought it was a compliment, but
I didn't mean it as a compliment. Steve Tyler is nothing but Aerosmith; that is his world. He is not a good
father; he's a guy with other interests in life. His only
life is that band.

What he's capable of doing now, I don't know. He
still hasn't gotten in touch with himself. He's missing
that element. I see this well-polished diamond, and it
stays a lump of coal. I think the work he's done in
the past few years is more commercial than creative.
I think he's put himself in a place from which he can't
move forward. You listen to Soundgarden and Alice
in Chains and Nine Inch Nails, and that's not alternative; that is rock and roll, that is what rock and roll
is now. It's not Led Zeppelin anymore, it's a whole
new supernova of its own. Maybe Aerosmith will figure out a way to do one big, final blast for an end
run. Isn't that what artists are supposed to do? I hope
they add more glory to their story, I really do. I still

listen to their records. I still get a thrill out of *Live
Bootleg*. They were a great kickass band. They still
are.

Could Steven and I ever be friends again? I think
we could, but he would have to make tremendous
changes. He would have to become a person. I don't
care that he's the lead singer of Aerosmith. I'm glad
he is, and I can put that in its proper place, in its little
niche, but I'd like to see Steven as a person. If he
made a magic transformation, would I have an affair
with him? I'd try to avoid it, but yeah, probably.
Oops, my guardian angel just hit me on the head. I
felt his wing bop me when I said that.

Would I marry him again? No way.

We were together so long, and in many ways he's
still the same person I don't like. Some people find
him very generous and caring and loving. And I say,
"Right. And how much are you being paid?" When
you're with him, you actually pay the price by giving
up a lot of yourself. If you don't have a lot of yourself
to give in the first place, then maybe you are getting
something from him.

He doesn't think he's being cheap with me and his
daughter; he really doesn't.

What could he do to surprise and delight me at this
point? Turn into a decent human being, about which
I think he has no clue. Make Mia and me not embarrassed that he's related to us. Not make us have to
fake it and do that Hollywood thing. Make it where
Mia could genuinely say, "God, my dad's great, he
calls me all the time to see how I am." I hate to say

it's only money or material items, but sometimes those things mean that someone is thinking about you, and with Steve that's pretty much the only way he shows it. I mean, she gets plenty of advice from me and she hates it. She needs her rich daddy to behave like one, and to behave like a gentleman.

As for me, creatively I'm completely dwarfed because I had to stop and raise my child. I would have liked to pursue the study of acting. There's a new school of acting out there. I wish I could be part of it. I physically and emotionally could not withstand the trauma of Aerosmith and Steven Tyler. It is the worst thing for any human being to go through. It makes me feel a kinship with all abused women. I don't care if the abused woman is so rich that she's sitting on a yacht; she's identical to the abused woman in a trailer park somewhere.

A woman has to know when to get out. A woman who has money has that advantage. It's easier for her to leave. I think that now I would walk out at the first sign that someone was going to break me down emotionally and physically. If a person is being abused, male or female, he or she has to leave. Abuse is a sin against the spirit.

I was so immature when I was with Steven. I never got to grow up. I was living in New York City and having a fine and dandy time. What did I have to do? Actors and artists have this network in New York, and people tend to take care of you, fluff you up, and offer you up to the gods. I was not strong, and I'm so afraid of not being strong now that it keeps me from having another relationship. I think the drugs and being with somebody who was so insane, opening doors that never should have been opened, seeing things I never should have seen, violent and twisted, maniacal behavior, all depleted my spirit so much that I was reduced to less than a person. I was in a kind of prison.

I'm just coming out of it. This is the first year I've realized I'm a woman, owning womanliness. I've had a growth spurt. Not having had a father myself, I had poor judgment when it came to men. Lack of knowledge. I didn't have a role model. I dedicated my entire life to my daughter because I didn't want to make another mistake and have her become part of another negative relationship. I didn't want her to have a bad stepfather, I didn't want her to have someone around who might say something to her that shouldn't be said. I was really afraid of that. I really, selfishly, wanted to be alone with my child to make up for what I didn't have with my mother, and I didn't want to make another mistake by having a male in the house who was bad.

I don't believe in telling your husband or boyfriend everything. I think that's what girlfriends are for. I like the fact that most guys don't tell girls everything. I like that separateness. Because we don't understand each other. We're really different. I think there are some things you share with your girlfriends, and some things you share with your guy. I don't think guys are really capable of understanding women, and women shouldn't even try to be understood by men. Respect and manners are very important. Very.

EIGHTEEN

Mia's Sister, the Movie Star

My daughter's half-sister, Liv Tyler, is very much in the spotlight these days, and I suppose it is expected of me to include her in this book, since she is a newly famous member of the astonishing Tyler family.

Steven and Liv's mother, Bebe Buell Shivers (who is also the off-and-on manager of Liv's career), had a fling of sorts in 1976 before and during Aerosmith's first European tour. Bebe was a very pretty girl and a Ford model until Ford dumped her for doing a *Playboy* spread. I heard that after her "moment" with Steven, Bebe came back looking like she'd been to war. It took a while for her to get back to being the beautiful Bebe. I can attest that he can do that to a girl.

Steven told me that he had sex with Bebe because Mick Jagger did it with Bebe. I always wondered if he really wanted to sleep with Mick. Steven said that he would have paid for Bebe to have an abortion if she'd wanted one, but I assume she wanted the baby.

I think she's done a brilliant job with her daughter's career. Bebe has turned out to be a shrewd business-woman, and I admire her for that.

Bebe and I have never fought over "Steven's love," whatever that might be, nor have we ever been close friends. I have nothing against her, and my fags are always telling me that Bebe and I should start having lunches and being girlfriends and all. I'm not sure that's what I want to do. Bebe is okay, but we just don't know each other very well. Our daughters are sisters and very fond of each other, and it's important that Bebe and I not be enemies. There is a bond be-tween us, whether I like it or not. But she has her own agenda and her own outlook on life, and they are so different from mine, not better or worse, just different. We don't see things the same way.

A psychic once told Bebe that she and I had been sisters in another life. Perhaps that is why Bebe is always so interested in what I'm doing. I went to see the same psychic to see what other gems he could come up with. He told me not only that we had been sisters, but that she had tried to kill me because I got some guy she wanted! Then I showed the psychic a picture of Steven and his new family, and he told me the guy was an "asshole" (they *never* use that word!) and that I should have nothing whatsoever to do with him. This was well after our divorce.

The story of the discovery of Liv's patrimony has been told in just about every magazine in the world, but there are different versions of it. Bebe remembers

it one way, Steven another, and my recollections may
not jibe with their recollections. So be it—I can tell
it only from my experiences and my point of view.

Here's how I watched it unfold: Every once in a
while, Steven would send for Mia to come watch him
perform. Once when Mia was eight and we were living in New Hampshire, Steven had his sister pick Mia
up and bring her to the concert in Boston. Steven was
going through one of his occasional "I've got to see
my daughter!" moments. Fine with me.

Mia came home from the show and told me she
had met this little girl backstage who was ten years
old, and someone had said, "My, my! You two look
just like sisters."

Now, this was not the first time I had heard of the
existence of a little girl who *might* have been Bebe's
daughter by Steven. I had known Bebe since the
Max's Kansas City days, and I knew that she had had
an affair with Steven. By this time (1987), she had
been living with Todd Rundgren, and the two of them
were bringing up a daughter. In fact, Todd's name
was on Liv's birth certificate. But Steven had told me
that Bebe had been showing up at his concerts with
a certain alarming regularity, always with this little
girl in tow. She never said anything to Steven like
"This is your daughter!" because she wasn't sure,
though she suspected, and it would have been uncool
for her to confront him like that.

Steven said that Bebe had given him a photograph
of her daughter when she was very little, and on one

of his visits he showed it to me and asked me if she looked like him. I said, "You, Mick," and I named a few more of Bebe's amours. He never brought it up again.

So when Mia told me about this look-alike, the wheels started turning and I asked her what the little girl's name was, and she couldn't remember.

Then I said, "What was her mommy's name?"

"Err . . ."

"Was it Bebe?"

And Mia shouted, "Yes! Bebe, that's her mommy's name!" And the possibility of it just flashed in my mind.

It was time for a you-better-sit-down-kid talk. I said something like, "You know, Daddy had lots of girl-friends before me, and even girlfriends while he was with me, and it's possible that he is the father of an-other little girl who could be about ten years old." She exclaimed, "Yippee! Now I have a sister!" I asked Mia what her daddy did when someone said that she and the other girl looked just like sisters. She said that Steven just got up and walked away.

Some stories say Steven owned up to being the father of Liv when she was ten years old, but that is not true. It didn't happen for four more years.

When I moved back to New York in 1991, I ran into Bebe and Liz Derringer, and Bebe said, "Oh, you have to come over and meet Liv! You just must!" It was like, we're both mothers of young daughters, I'll show you mine and you show me yours. In the meantime, Mia and Liv had met a few more times at concerts, but nothing more was said about them being sisters, certainly not by Steven.

I went to Bebe's apartment in the West 20's, and I just looked at this girl and tears welled up in my eyes. I mean, this was my daughter's sister. Liv wasn't tall and thin then, she was still short, and the two girls were like two little buttery balls, two healthy New England–type kids. I didn't say, "This is Steven's daughter." I said, "This is Mia's sister."

I wasn't crying for myself, and certainly not for Steven, but for Mia. All of a sudden Mia had a sister. I was thrilled. And I could tell that Bebe seemed very satisfied with my display of emotion.

There was no doubt in Bebe's mind now. Bebe had started taking pictures of Liv dressed like Steven, with the sunglasses and scarves, but she needed something better than that to get him to admit to his responsibilities. I said to Bebe, "You had better do something," and she said, "Well, you know, I want to make friends with him," and I suspected she wanted to get back with him, get rid of the second wife and be his third. That would be fabulous for her.

Bebe had the nerve to say to me, "That wasn't much of a marriage you had, you know." Well, fuck her for that. I was still in litigation with him. I had nine years with this person and she had maybe three weeks. Why was she being nasty to me? I was not the other woman in his life anymore. He had a new wife. She wanted people to know her daughter was a

Tyler, because Tyler was now cool again. All I cared about was that my daughter had a sister.

As for Todd, he was over. He was extremely upset that Bebe was pursuing this patrimony possibility with Steven, and he was asking for a return of all the money he had put out over the last fourteen years which supported Bebe and Liv. But I knew Steven, and I told Bebe, "You better see a lawyer, because he is not going to do anything for you and your child." Bebe didn't want to follow that route. She couldn't understand why anyone wouldn't want to love her daughter as much as she did, but this was not Steven's way, and I tried to convince her of that.

"I want to do it peacefully," she said. "I'd like him to come forward."

I replied, "He's never going to come forward and give you anything."

"Well, my relationship with him is more friendly," Bebe continued.

"It just goes to show how much you don't know this guy," I explained.

Despite all of the dangling of Liv that Bebe did in front of Steven, he was not about to "come forward." So she decided maybe she did need a lawyer. Also, she was tired of working two jobs. Then on TV I saw that attorney Raoul Felder had represented some girl in a paternity suit against Desi Arnaz, Jr., and I thought, *Well, there's a good lawyer for this case.* So Bebe went to Raoul Felder.

When Steven heard this, he got very pissed off.

This was four years after our divorce, to keep the time frame straight. He called me in a rage: "Why don't you mind your own fucking business? Why did you say anything to her?" Because I'm sure Bebe said to Steven, "Oh, Cyrinda is sure that Liv is Mia's sister," or "They look so much alike, they must be sisters," or something like that.

I shot back, "Fuck you, our daughter has a sister. She's always wanted a sister, and now it's clear she has one, and you're not worming out of this one." And sure enough, Bebe's lawyer got a court order for a blood test. Steven showed up with his own lawyer and his business manager and his bodyguards, and Liv was there with her mother. He had his blood taken, and then they put the needle in Liv's arm, and her blood went spurting all over. Steven didn't even say anything, he just got up with his entourage and stomped out. I don't care what version the Hollywood press agents are telling now, this was very traumatic for Liv and very unpleasant. She couldn't believe he didn't offer to take her out for a soda or something.

I've got to hand it to Bebe. She was chumming for great white shark, and she'd thrown out lots of big chunks, and she got him. The blood test came back and confirmed Steven as Liv's biological father, and Bebe changed Liv's name and started presenting her as the star of the future.

Steven was up to his ears in conflict over this. He felt he had to explain it to Mia, but he still wanted to avoid the whole issue. He didn't become Liv's adoring father until she started getting into the spotlight by her own merits. I just saw him on TV where he was at this party in South Beach for some magazine that featured Liv on the cover, and he's going, "This is a hip magazine, it's alive, it's fresh." He's doing the Hollywood thing, and he's so bad at it; he's so phony. I thought he was a jerk for not admitting paternity until he took the blood test.

Mia was thrilled with the whole situation. It was the greatest thing that had ever happened to her. She finally had a sister. It got off to a bit of a rough start, though. You know, one girl is fourteen and the other is twelve, and these are not wise and savvy women. At the beginning Liv was going, "Oh, I look so much more like Steven than you do!" and this kind of bullshit was way out of Mia's league. She had never dealt with anyone who has attitude. Mia started to hate her and didn't want anything to do with her. She would make me tell Steven that she wouldn't go someplace if Liv was going to be there. Mia had been crying for years over the neglect she'd gotten from her father, and now there was this added pressure.

There was a lot of friction between all the grown-ups at that point. Bebe hated Steven's new wife. People were acting ridiculous, and that's what bothered me. All these adults were acting like children and never thinking about the kids. I saw two innocent children in the middle of a bunch of disgusting, child-ish, mean, nasty, selfish adults. Steven made this child, Liv. And if we're only talking about money, he has a lot of it. It's his responsibility.

Oddly, things got better between the two girls when Liv's career started to take off. And I think Liv started to see that not only her mother, but also her father was homing in on her game. Also, it's become apparent to her how limited her father is emotionally. I remember Liv was in my apartment once, and Steven came over, and it was just after the paternity question was settled. She was literally jumping on him like a big Irish setter, and he was looking at me like, "Help!" I just sat there and stared, even though I felt bad for the girls. He's trying to untangle Liv from around his neck, Mia is jealous, and no one is happy except me. I loved it.

According to the newspapers, Steven says that he's so close to Liv that he can't even say what they talk about. As if she talks to him about sex or boyfriends. You've got to be kidding me. Does he think she wants fatherly advice from a sex addict, some half-baked crispy critter who goes to a hospital for sex addiction therapy?

The sisters are really close now. They're on the phone all the time. Mia is really proud of Liv, and she's thrilled about Liv's stardom. The father-daughter stuff is nauseating, though, and they both know it. There was a gossip item in the *New York Post* about Liv firing Bebe, and some unidentified insider said that it's Steven, not Bebe, "who's cashing in on his kid." Then another insider said that for the first ten years of her life, Steven didn't want anything to do with Liv. (That proves I wasn't the insider, because it was fourteen years.) And the insider went on to say that now Steven's prancing around with Liv at her premieres, and that Steven is the one Liv ought to fire. I swear, it wasn't me who said that. The feeling must be universal.

EPILOGUE
Resurfacing

There is no such thing as a total divorce when there are children involved. Those marriages last forever, in some form or other, no matter what legal, physical, financial, or emotional twists are applied to them.

Steven and I seem to have gone through some spiral passage, and now we've emerged on an entirely different level. After all the abuse, I'm a princess again whenever we're together. He's respectful, almost playful, even when we're going at each other full tilt via lawyers, faxes, phone, or in person. We were lovers and partners, and now we're Opponents (that capital O is certainly intentional), and that's part of the fate of this very odd couple. The end of the struggle is nowhere in sight.

When we first met, we challenged each other—it was an unspoken challenge, but a powerful one. I thought I was his saving grace, a touch of class he badly needed. He was my Prince Valiant. He was, and is, extremely talented—certainly better at his work than I was at mine. But I had the panache, so, together I thought we'd be perfect.

What happens when you make important life decisions based on superficial criteria? You fuck up, that's what, and that's what we did. I was overwhelmed by his sexiness, his musical abilities, and of course the high-flying glamour of it all. But I didn't know him, I didn't know how sick he was, mentally and emotionally. I had never been around anyone that damaged, or maybe I never took the time to be around anyone long enough to find out. By the time I found out where I'd put myself, I was an abused wife, a mother, and a full-blown drug addict. I could have gone completely under, but I fought my way back up. That was some dive I took.

I'm always asked: If I had it to do all over again, what would I have done? How can I answer that? Then I wouldn't have my child, whom I love more than anything else in the world. I'd like to have made those early years more comfortable for her, but that's all I'd change. Somehow I picked the wrong guy and got the right child.

Right now I like being free. I think being liberated is a wonderful goal. I think marriage and poverty are clearly not liberating, nor is fame. Knowledge is the most liberating thing you can have, whether it's from a book or a museum or a concert or the street. I made lots of mistakes that were painful and very hard to live through. I wish I had gotten a real first-class education, because I might have focused more on a career. I still have a fantasy about being a fabulous magazine editor.

I guess that right now I'm the New York woman I wanted to be since I was a teenager—although when you're seventeen, you don't know that forty is going to be a little more complicated. I'm living on the Upper East Side. I still would like to lose some weight and have more money. I'm constantly school-shopping for my daughter. I have a fax machine and a cell phone, both of which I use a lot, and I'm struggling with the joys of operating a computer. I have a great acupuncturist and fully intend to visit the New York Zen Center, which is right around the corner, but it's so hard to find the time. I'm glad Central Park is nearby; sometimes just seeing a tree makes things better. Someday I'd like a little place in the country to visit on weekends, but not in New Hampshire.

I saw Dee Dee Ramone at a party a few weeks ago, and he was so sweet. He said, "Hello, Cyrinda," and I said, "Hello, Dee Dee," and he said, "Would you please sit on my face?" He said it in such a nice way. I always thought he was a gentleman in spite of his roguish reputation. I said, "Well, not today, Dee Dee, but it's nice to see you anyway," and he said, "So nice to see you, too!" I guess this is a good place to mention the fact that I have not "been" with a man in seven years. Mr. Right, if and when he ever comes along, is going to have to meet some pretty high standards.

Jerry Lee Lewis played at Tramps one night, and I went with my lawyer Jay Butterman and friends, and it was so great. This is truly rock and roll, the real rock and roll like the songs in my brother's record collection, the music that was the most glorious thing in my whole childhood. I got a little teary-eyed during the show. Jerry Lee's in his sixties now, and he's still the Killer, but there was something about seeing him that told me my childhood was over.

After the show I was thinking, *Boy, despite living the way he lived, all the drugs, the hotels, the wives, the scandals, the violence, the cigarettes, the dramas and the traumas and all that, he's still sexy.* Hmm . . . I wonder what it would be like to hang out with Jerry Lee?

ACKNOWLEDGMENTS

I'd like to thank all the people who kept me believing there is hope, love, and trust: Mia, Virginia Clayton, HSH Antoine de Lobkowicz, Michael Baldridge, Todd Gribben, Anne Katomski, Scott Peper, Brian, Ali and Alex Simineau, Bandit, Boxer, Oliver, the Count, Genie and Geri, Beth and Patty, Randi Reisfeld, Legs McNeil, Charles Krewsen, Kevin Mc-Shane, and Jay Butterman.

To all the people in this book: Thank you for being part of my life, for better or for worse.

To Julia Hasz, Mia's cousin: If you read this, please let us know that you're okay.

Special thanks to Danny Fields for helping me see things in a brighter shade of bright, to all the musical greats for giving me direction through their art, and to Auntie Mame for proclaiming, "Life is a banquet, and most poor suckers are starving to death." My sentiments exactly.

C.F.T.